short narrative book one by dave mckean ©2000

Arch itect etype

1. In the beginning, somebody around here created the chicken and the egg.

2. And low, the earth was null and void and the darkness was dark, and the deepness was deep, and the waters broke and all of that palaver.

3. And oh my God, let there be a light bulb. And the egg cracked and the chicken croaked and would you believe it? There was indeed a light bulb.

4. And we all stood around the light bulb, and, you know, gave it a prod, and said, "Is it any good?"

5. And agreeing that it would probably do for the moment we called the light bulb our brain-child.
Our conception.
Our new wrinkle.
And someone says "Let's call it a day."

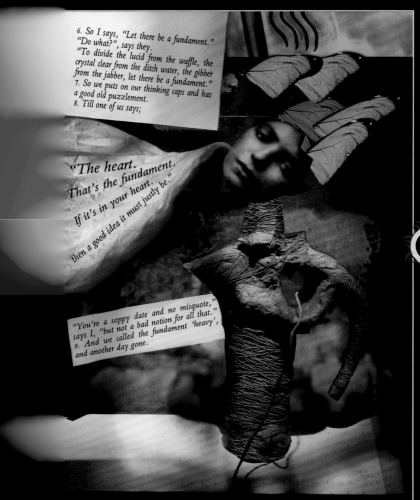

6. So I says, "Let there be a fundament."
"Do what?", says they.
"To divide the lucid from the waffle, the crystal clear from the ditch water, the gibber from the jabber, let there be a fundament."

7. So we puts on our thinking caps and has a good old puzzlement.

8. Till one of us says;

"The heart.
That's the fundament.
If it's in your heart.
then a good idea it must justly be."

"You're a soppy date and no misquote," says I, "but not a bad notion for all that."

9. And we called the fundament 'heavy', and another day gone.

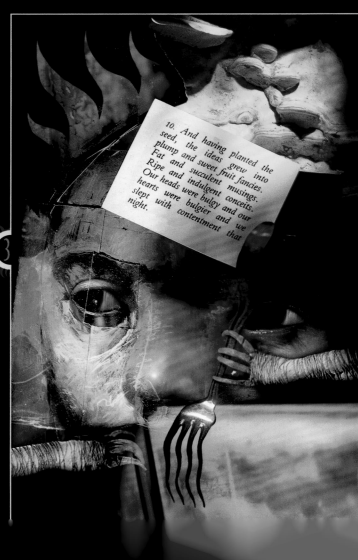

10. And having planted the seed, the ideas grew into plump and sweet fruit fancies. Fat and succulent musings. Ripe and indulgent conceits. Our heads were bulgy and our hearts were bulgier and we slept with contentment that night.

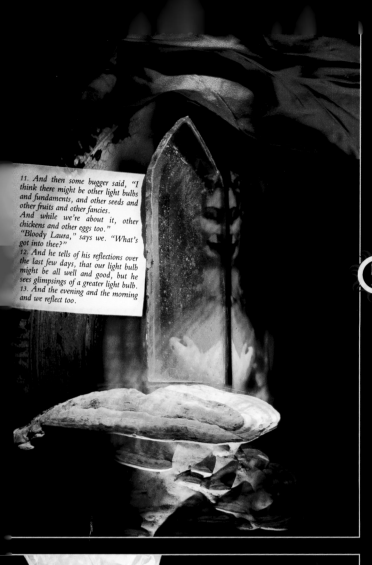

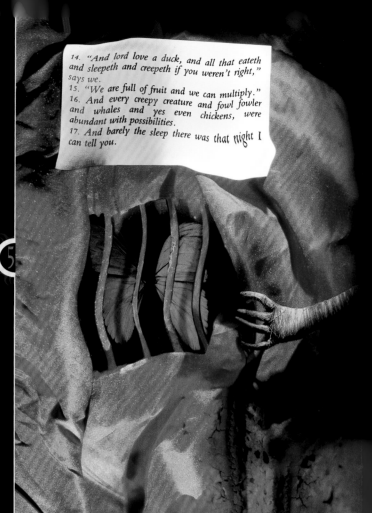

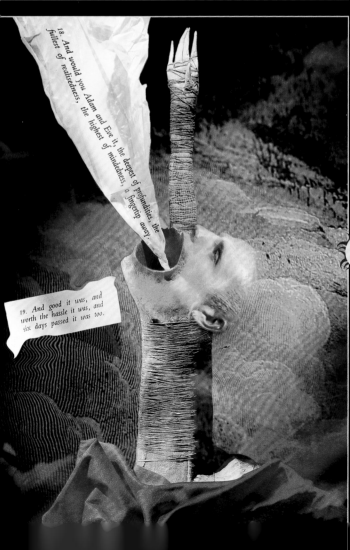

This first edition of

PICTURES THAT TICK

BOOK ONE

By DAVE McKEAN

is limited to four thousand copies

and is designed by Dave McKean

Editorial pages typeset in Typographiction [T-26]

All stories ©2001 Dave McKean

Printed in Hong Kong

through Interpress, Ltd.

Other publications by Dave McKean

COMIX

Cages: a comic novel
1998
Slow Chocolate Autopsy [with Iain Sinclair]
1998
Voodoo Lounge [with The Rolling Stones]
1996
Buckethead [with Buckethead]
1995
Mr. Punch [with Neil Gaiman]
1995
Signal To Noise [with Neil Gaiman]
1992
Arkham Asylum [with Grant Morrison]
1989
Black Orchid [with Neil Gaiman]
1988
Violent Cases [with Neil Gaiman]
1987

PHOTOGRAPHY MONOGRAPHS

The Particle Tarot : The Minor Arcana
2002
The Particle Tarot : The Major Arcana
2000
Option : Click
1998
A Small Book Of Black & White Lies
1995

CHILDRENS BOOKS

The Wolves in the Walls [with Neil Gaiman]
2002
Coraline [with Neil Gaiman]
2001
The Day I Swapped My Dad For Two Goldfish [with Neil Gaiman]
1997

DESIGN, ILLUSTRATION AND PHOTOGRAPHY

Landor's Tower [by Iain Sinclair]
2001
What's Welsh For Zen : The Autobiography of John Cale
1999
The Cafe Des Amis Postcard Set
1998
The Anthropomorphik Calendar
1997
The Tip Of My Tongue
1995
The Vertigo Tarot [with Rachel Pollack]
1995
Wizard & Glass [by Stephen King]
1995

RETROSPECTIVE MONOGRAPH

Complicity
2002

Published by Hourglass . Allen Spiegel Fine Arts

Hourglass fax: [uk 44] 1797 270030

ASFA Tel / Fax: [us 1] 831 372 4672

221 Lobos Avenue

Pacific Grove

California

93950

email: asfa@redshift.com

www.allenspiegelfinearts.com

ISBN 0-9642069-5-1

This book is dedicated to my family:

My mother Nora

Clare of course

My co-writers on a couple of the shorts, Yolanda and Liam

Thanks also to:

Allen Spiegel

Maria Cullis

Victoria

Tim Hobday

Kent Williams

The Residents

CONTENTS

1
SMALL TITLE
2
ARCHITECT/ARCHETYPE
5
READY
7
CONTENTS
9
TWO PANELS 1
11
TWO PANELS 2
13
TWO PANELS 3
14
ASH

25
MIXED METAPHORS
[First published in Morning, Japan and le Cheval Sans Téte, France]
36
BLACK WATER
44
LIAM'S STORY
46
YOL'S STORY
48
THE THING ABOUT TRAVEL
49
TWO PAGES
[First published in Windows No. 1, USA]
52
👁

101
BITTEN AND BRUISED
[First published as a Bedeteca 5th. anniversary edition, Lisbon]
134
YOUR CLOTHES ARE DEAD
143
LILLIE
[First published in Freak Show, USA]
151
THE TRUTH IS SPOKEN HERE
[First published in A-1, USA]
160
DAWN
169
HIS STORY
[First published in Bento No. 1, USA]
183
UNDER/NORMAL/OVER

Cover: PICTURES THAT TICK [Model: Maria Cullis]

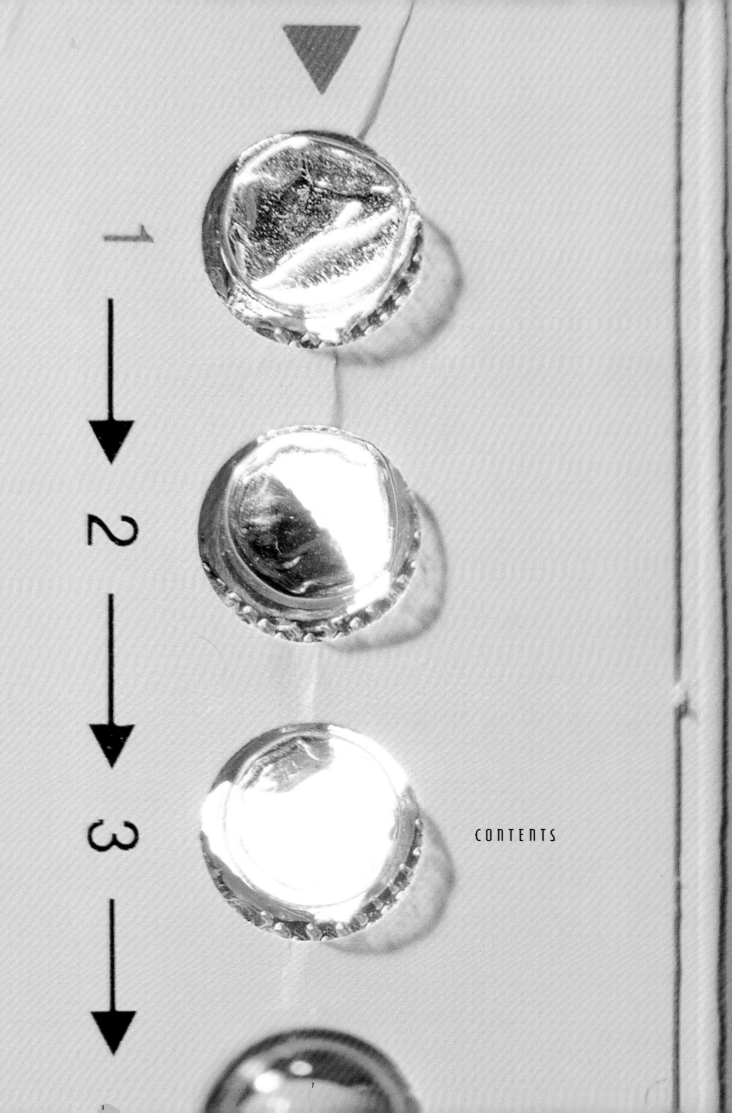

1 ➝

2 ➝

3 ➝

CONTENTS

14
one page comix

15

frustrated with elaboration

stayed up one night daubing on photographs with ink and acrylic

no reference

no reason

fun

-

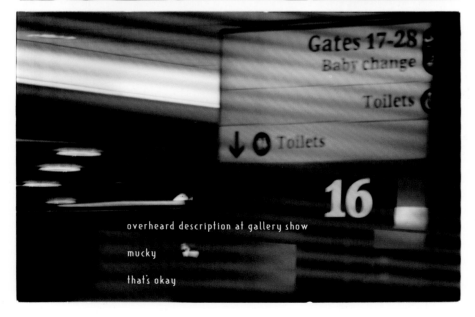

wet image

emulsion scraped off in layers

paint sits on surface

dries quickly

layers build

16

overheard description at gallery show

mucky

that's okay

All the people I admire can fly —

Why can't I do that?

it seems i have an exhibition of comix in majorca
majorca
yes i thought that too
but sitting on the plane as the sun sinks into the sea
drinking my freixenet
i'm thinking
this is a great job
comix really is a wibbly wobbly world all of its own
-
over the past few years i've been working on other things
[i slipped a few pages of comix into john cale's autobiography and into projects for iain sinclair and kodak, but]
i've mostly been making films photography illustration and design for cds books ads and assorted other
and i've missed comix
but not really the business of comix
-
when my first book with neil gaiman was published comix were scrabbling up the hill of respectability
and then they were the new pop music
and then comix boomed and busted
and then tv chefs and interior decorators and typographers all enjoyed their fifteen minutes in the charts
and comix fell back down the hill again and came to rest in a sort of intermediate marketing tool twilight zone
a place for developing daft movies
and toys
-
these few years distance have afforded me a stripped down clearer view of it all
and the results are in
and the conclusions are fairly straight forward
one - wasn't winsor mccay just great?
i mean
great
two - there have been an extraordinary number of completely redundant deadends
three - unlike the music industry which feels to me like a hyper active rubics cube obsessive
[bloody hell the colours are the same but they're all in a slightly different order now wow it's gonna be huge]
the comix industry seems to be pathologically afraid of change
four - is there a visual narrative medium more powerful accessible intimate democratic than comix?
i don't think so
plays need a theatre
narrative art needs a narrative gallery
tv needs money
film needs considerably more money and two hundred and thirty seven lunches
comix need a pen
some paper
maybe a photo copier
a friendly printer
i'll just assume because you are reading this in a comic that you have actively bought or borrowed
that you are positively inclined toward the expressive power and personal intimacy that comix can achieve
but here's another one
everybody does comix
i mean everybody
everybody takes holiday photos yes?
or wedding photos
or shots of the kids
everyone uses them to tell stories
recalling an event in sequential order
telling the story of a life
birth till graduation
it's one of the things to make you go hmmm isn't it?
-

My parents fight —

The street is quiet.

so back to the plane
i will do the press and the tv thing
and talk about my stuff via an interpreter
[inviting him to translate slow chocolate autopsy]
and the kind people who are looking after me
and putting me where i'm supposed to be
will bitch about their own comix industry
and i will say well in england we don't have one
and they will say neither do we
and then show me gorgeous books published by edicions de ponent ediciones sinsentido
small passionate spanish publishers
and i will get the passion back for comix
that i felt when i was twelve
-
maybe i should have done this book ten years ago when i first made notes for it
but i didn't need it then
i need it now
i've never enjoyed making comix so much as with the short shorts captured in this book
as with cages
[a longer story published as a novel in 1998]
i've tried to make a book that i would buy
and that i think is missing from comic store racks
and that's about it
-
oh while doing the press thing
sitting in a silver and black sleek office inside sanostra [obra social i cultural]
one of the journos asked me why my work was so dark
a common question so i guess it must be there
but i just don't see it really
that's just the way i feel about the world
i looked past the grey haired chap with his black jacket
metal tape machine and charcoal pencil
through the window to the glorious sunny palmy orange tree almondy february afternoon in palma
[the next day i left blue skies and turquoise sea behind me
clouds slowly gathered
i flew back into gatwick airport through a snow storm]
maybe i'd feel differently about the world if i lived here

dave mckean
on a plane
no really
2001

There's a woman on tv. I try and empathise with her situation.

I can't.

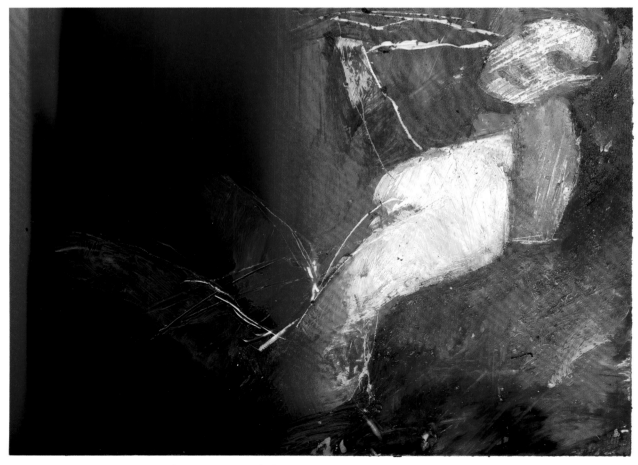

I'll try again when I'm older.

ash

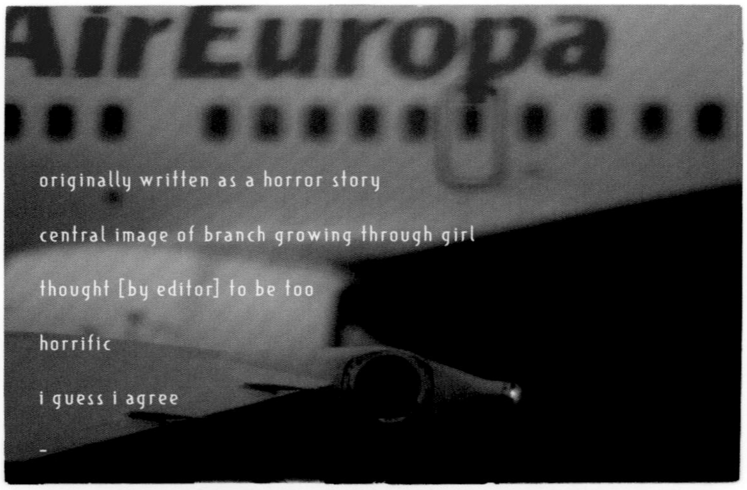

originally written as a horror story

central image of branch growing through girl

thought [by editor] to be too

horrific

i guess i agree

_

but the image is right

[i tried to dull it down]

but it touches all the sensitive nerves

the rawness of emotion at that age

so i guess it's right

[thinks]

...

ASH

There once, and once only,
was a little girl called Ash.

And Ash fell asleep one night,
and one night only, and in the
morning, awoke and lived...

THE END.

What?

You want more than that?

Like what?

You want to know something about her?
Well...
Okay.

Ash lived in the woods, in a house in the woods.
Mostly in her bedroom, in a house, in the woods.
With her father, and her stepmother.

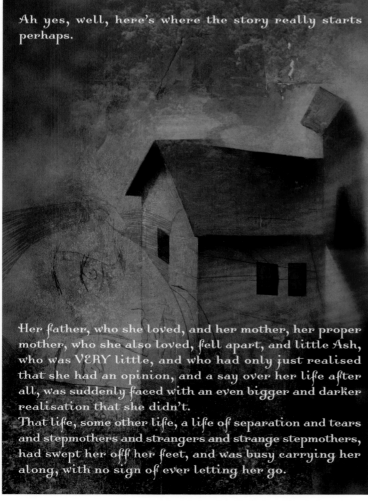

Ah yes, well, here's where the story really starts perhaps.

Her father, who she loved, and her mother, her proper mother, who she also loved, fell apart, and little Ash, who was VERY little, and who had only just realised that she had an opinion, and a say over her life after all, was suddenly faced with an even bigger and darker realisation that she didn't.
That life, some other life, a life of separation and tears and stepmothers and strangers and strange stepmothers, had swept her off her feet, and was busy carrying her along, with no sign of ever letting her go.

And this made little Ash very sad.
And angry.
And spiteful.
And full of fear.

And so little Ash fell asleep one night, and one night only, and in the morning, awoke and lived...

THE END

What, you want even more than that?
Aren't you tired yet? Aren't you ready to go to sleep?
Oh well...
Alright...

Little Ash fell asleep, but just before she fell asleep, her stepmother - who was thought by some people, some little people, to be wicked, and was thought by some other people, some other paternal people who were loved by the little people, to be really rather wonderful and if only they'd met ten years ago - read little Ash a story.

And the story was short and simple and developed quite steadily, and insinuated its way into little Ash as she slept, crawling over her white skin, rooting where it could find shelter,

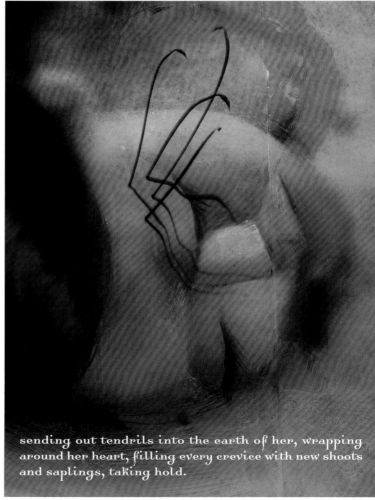

sending out tendrils into the earth of her, wrapping around her heart, filling every crevice with new shoots and saplings, taking hold.

And by the time little Ash realised what was happening, it was too late.
She was part of the undergrowth, deep in the heart of the woods,
her life grew unchecked through the night.

And soon little Ash wasn't so little.
And she grew into her teenage years, carried along
by the momentum of her life, a life which thrusted out
before her, a path of least resistance, a foregone
conclusion, a chaotic inevitability,

and that same life, stretching out behind her,
an arterial trunk, umbilicle memories, her roots.

And Ash – who until recently was little, but who didn't like to be called little anymore, and who wouldn't acknowledge anyone who did – realised that her life was far bigger than her bedroom and her house, and even bigger than her father, who she still loved I suppose, but from whom she felt increasingly distanced.

Her life was as big as the woods.

By the time Ash was old enough to have forgotten her childhood name, she could see over the entire forest.
She never married.
She was not really in any position to marry.
She never had any children of her own.

And sometimes Ash wished she could change the life that grew through her, but these occasional thoughts were fruitless. She listened to the owls and the insects and enjoyed the view.

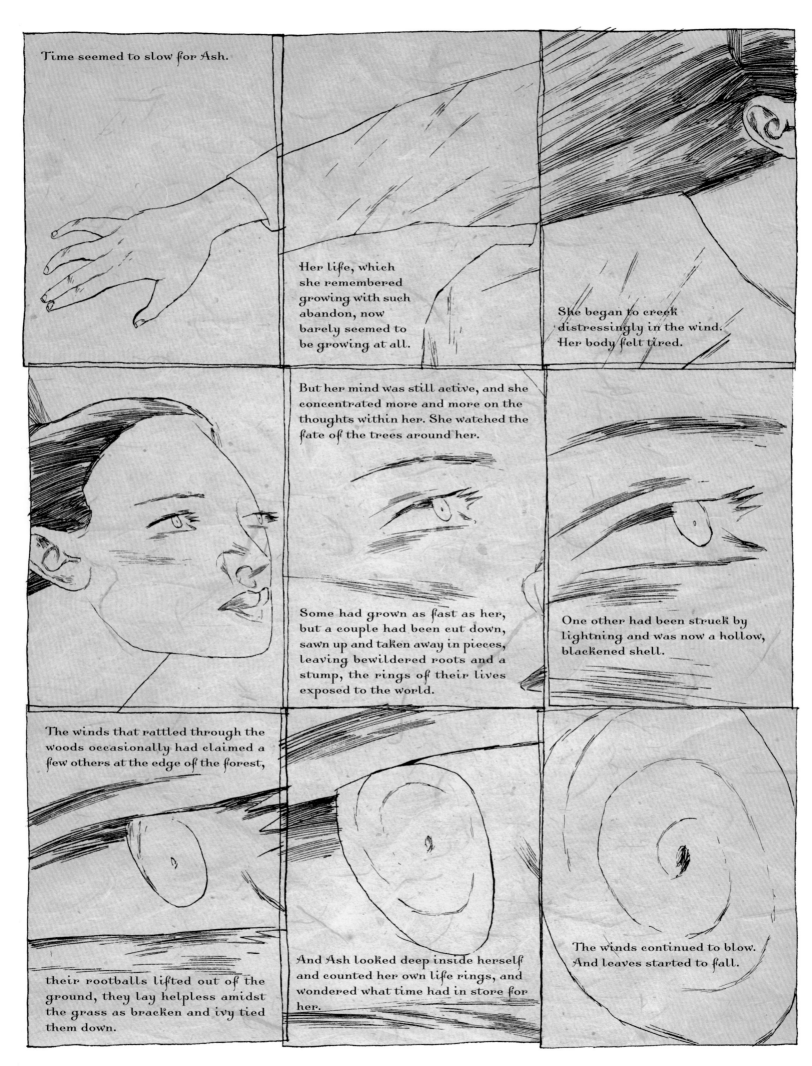

Time seemed to slow for Ash.

Her life, which she remembered growing with such abandon, now barely seemed to be growing at all.

She began to creak distressingly in the wind. Her body felt tired.

But her mind was still active, and she concentrated more and more on the thoughts within her. She watched the fate of the trees around her.

Some had grown as fast as her, but a couple had been cut down, sawn up and taken away in pieces, leaving bewildered roots and a stump, the rings of their lives exposed to the world.

One other had been struck by lightning and was now a hollow, blackened shell.

The winds that rattled through the woods occasionally had claimed a few others at the edge of the forest, their rootballs lifted out of the ground, they lay helpless amidst the grass as bracken and ivy tied them down.

And Ash looked deep inside herself and counted her own life rings, and wondered what time had in store for her.

The winds continued to blow. And leaves started to fall.

Ash spent more and more time with her eyes tight shut.

Looking through the layers of her life, travelling through the blood and sap of her life,

out to the tips of her branches, and occasionally –

though the hardness of her past discouraged her – back down the vast trunk of her life to the ground.

Looking through the layers of her life, And Ash saw the hearts of others who had lived lives very different to hers.

And Ash saw the parasites who had made their lives within her.

And deep, deep inside Ash found the wreckage of her bedroom, and her childhood,

and her father who she hadn't thought about for a long time, and the stepmother she had tried to forget, but who she realised ran through the very core of her life, the oldest and tightest and strongest life ring within her.

And Ash cried sweet sticky tears as the last of her leaves fell to earth, and a dull haze appeared on the horizon.

Ash opened her eyes and saw that the sky was now a
profound and endless ochre.
She felt cold. Her bones ached.
Her flesh creaked and flaked.

And Ash realised she was now very old indeed.

She touched her brittle bark skin, which crumbled
to dust, and her dry fibrous hair, which snapped
between her fingers.

And Ash felt alone and empty.

She looked out at the other trees, and she realised
that her life was one of thousands, any one of which
could have been her, she had grown wherever her
life had taken her, she had drifted wherever the wind
had blown her.

She had never had an opinion.
She had never had a say over her life.

And then she remembered. Way, way back. Back down the twisted, decaying branches, back into the gnarled and rotting roots, back before even the smallest tired tendrils, back to the seed of her life, the seed of THIS life. Back to little Ash.

Who had only just realised she did have an opinion, and a say over her life, before the resentment and bitterness had embedded themselves inside her. Before the feelings of her betrayal over the strange stepmother in her life, the intruder who had displaced her mother, the weed that had infested her house and even her bedroom, before all this hate, there could have been such a different life.

And as Ash finally understood that her life had died, and as the birds started to sing the sun above the edge of the world, little Ash awoke.
And lived...

And I think felt slightly different about things, and now it really is very late, and you have a busy day tomorrow,

so that is absolutely, and finally, the end.

mixed metaphors

made for japan
       never liked manga   [generally]

       except for the pauses   [   ]

       time allowed to watch the clouds

       otherwise – eyes grotesquely saucerous

       noses worryingly compressed

       apocalypse culture w/my little pony aesthetic

       –

story published in morning [japan]

and le cheval sans tête [france]

sparked by news from yugoslavia

different cultures formerly friends

forced to live apart – communicate in different language

MIXED METAPHORS

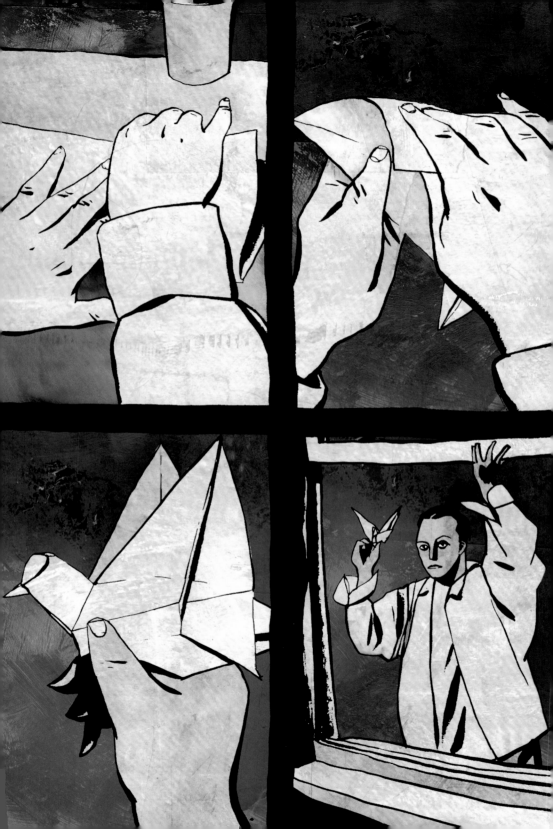

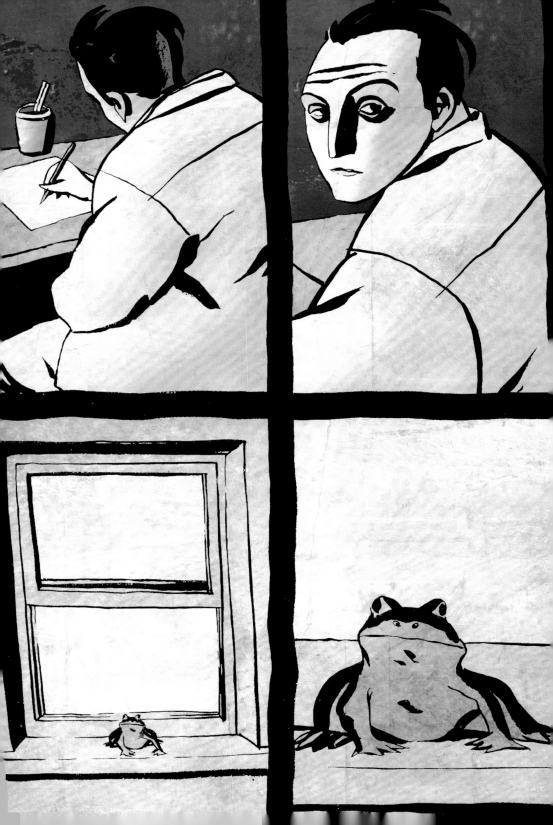

black water

moved to kent

the isle of oxney

the military canal

herons

–

just a thought

like a note to myself

drawn in a day [off]

left unfinished until now

always liked the fish

BLACK WATER

That a baby will become in merely a few years, a wrinkled bag of bones, seems as impossible as it becoming a tiger or a tree. HERACLITUS

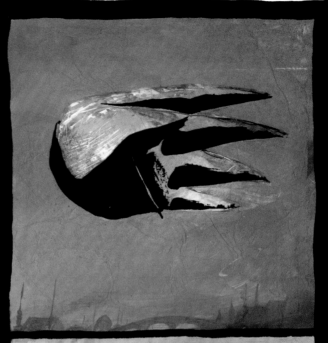

The line running through his hand had nearly ended.

He felt the pull of the river again. As a kid, when those first days of Spring lured him to the tributary near his house, he thought he'd always live here. Be happy here.

You should never return to water you knew as a child.
Jeremiah? Is that you?
The water you remembered has moved on . . .

Maybe the river feels that this is a more appropriate colour for this time. There are no children living nearby anymore.

Only myself and some other birds.

You're right, I shouldn't have come back.

Last September I stepped into my bedroom, opened the window wide, transformed myself, and flew away. I have never regretted it.

HILDESHEIMER

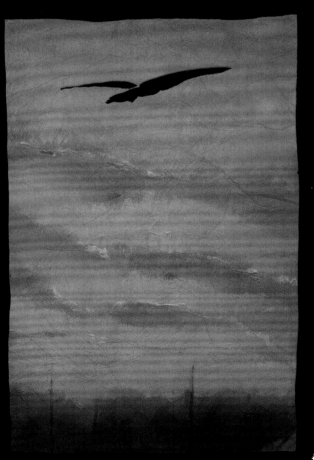

colour copiers

borrowed from my children

royalty statements for a four year old

oh dear

litigation

tense domestic situation

i'm sure it won't happen

-

fun with photo copiers

colour scans = time passes

built in narrative

yellow   magenta   cyan   black

rapid light fall-off as object is lifted away from the glass

wolf's breath is cotton wool

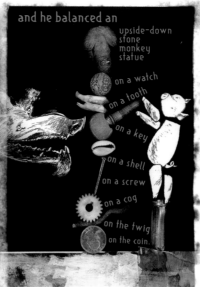

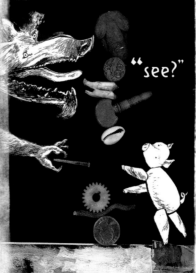

yol's story

she grew game plants in her front room

she played the i am the god of plant games game

she played the icarus and the sun flower game

she played the out of body experience game

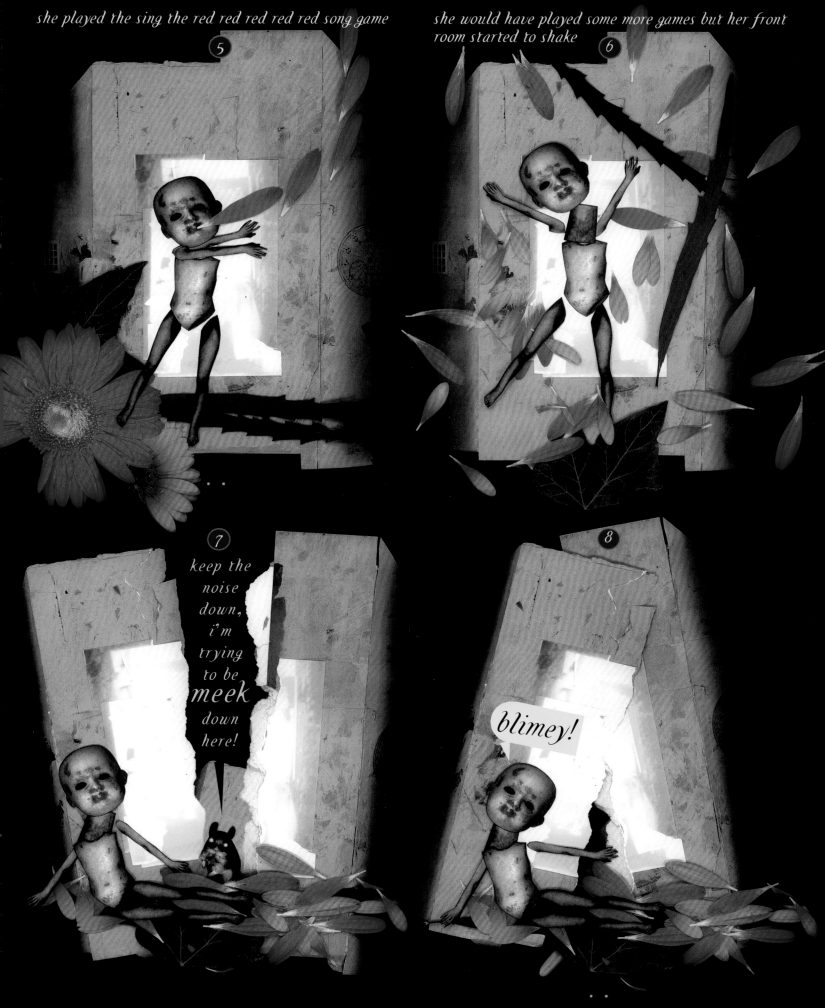

we'd go and visit friends
a long way away

we'd set sail in the morning

cross stormy seas
through the night

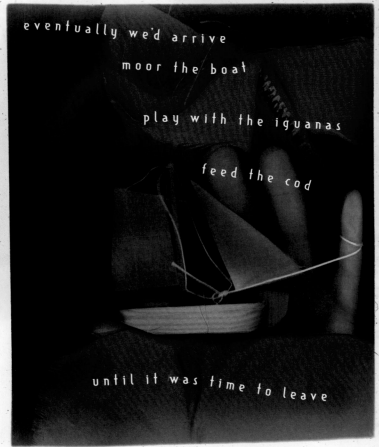

eventually we'd arrive

moor the boat

play with the iguanas

feed the cod

until it was time to leave

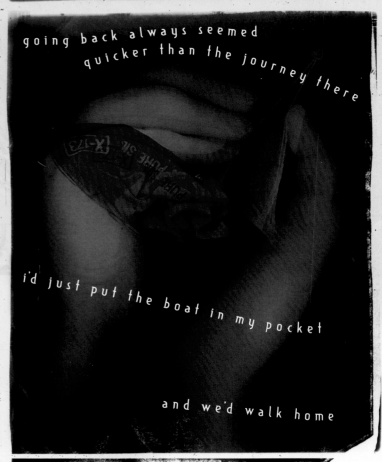

going back always seemed
quicker than the journey there

i'd just put the boat in my pocket

and we'd walk home

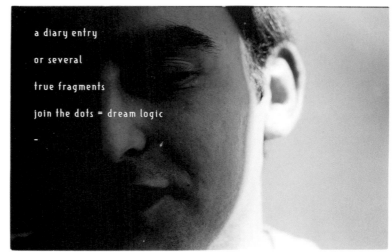

a diary entry

or several

true fragments

join the dots = dream logic

-

circus story forwarded by jonathan carrol

daily missives

email missiles

some funny silly some icky

must spend all his day surfing

how does he find the time

to write novels?

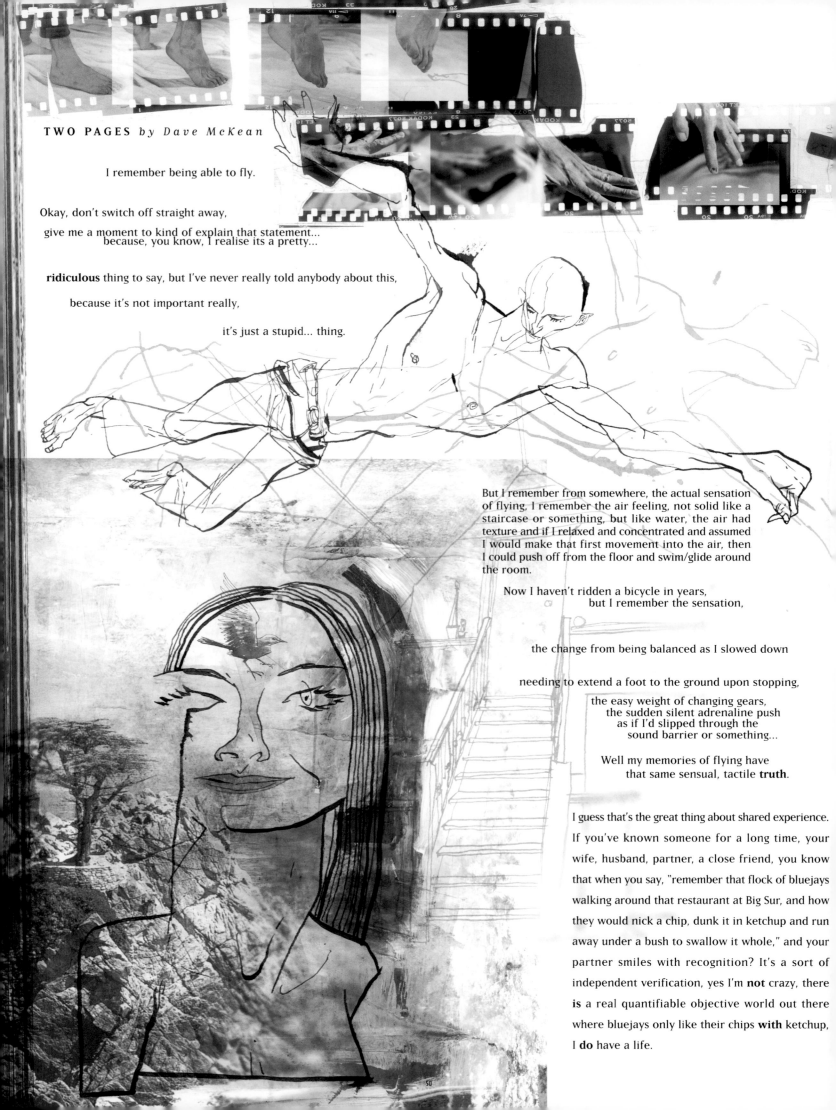

TWO PAGES *by Dave McKean*

I remember being able to fly.

Okay, don't switch off straight away,

give me a moment to kind of explain that statement...
because, you know, I realise its a pretty...

ridiculous thing to say, but I've never really told anybody about this,

because it's not important really,

it's just a stupid... thing.

But I remember from somewhere, the actual sensation of flying, I remember the air feeling, not solid like a staircase or something, but like water, the air had texture and if I relaxed and concentrated and assumed I would make that first movement into the air, then I could push off from the floor and swim/glide around the room.

Now I haven't ridden a bicycle in years,
but I remember the sensation,

the change from being balanced as I slowed down

needing to extend a foot to the ground upon stopping,
the easy weight of changing gears,
the sudden silent adrenaline push
as if I'd slipped through the
sound barrier or something...

Well my memories of flying have
that same sensual, tactile **truth**.

I guess that's the great thing about shared experience. If you've known someone for a long time, your wife, husband, partner, a close friend, you know that when you say, "remember that flock of bluejays walking around that restaurant at Big Sur, and how they would nick a chip, dunk it in ketchup and run away under a bush to swallow it whole," and your partner smiles with recognition? It's a sort of independent verification, yes I'm **not** crazy, there **is** a real quantifiable objective world out there where bluejays only like their chips **with** ketchup, I **do** have a life.

I went to this thing recently. I was dreading it really, but it turned out to be a wonderful experience, actually quite important to me in a way I can't seem to quantify. I've certainly thought about it several times since. I'm writing a film, and Channel 4 asked me to go to a lab for five days to workshop the script, talk about the future of TV/film in this country, and generally interact. The in-house producers and we invitees were all very different people with very different views, but something about the intensity of the environment, the fact that most people's work was very personal, mine certainly was - a story based around a friends suicide - something about the communal dinners and the ruthless sense of humour really made me feel connected to these people in a remarkably immediate way. As I say I can't really give the experience any rational, logical substance.

My film is as much about anecdote as anything else, people telling stories, some true, some not-so-, so I watched people very closely as they related to each other, and took part in the round table swapping of true-life bizarreness and embarrassing confessionals. Many included bodily functions of one sort or another. Some were just daft. I started to define these people by the stories they told and their reactions to others. I told my current favourite apparently true newspaper story:

So this circus dwarf died recently in a tragic accident during his troupes act that included jumping off a platform onto a trampoline and up onto another platform, various animals wandered around the edge... this was sort of a grand finalé type of thing. And this dwarf lost his footing slightly and jumped/fell off the platform, bounced on the trampoline, but at the edge so he came off at an angle, flew into the mouth of a hippopotamus which has an automatic swallow reflex, and the dwarf disappeared. The crowd went wild, huge applause, standing ovation... you know, they thought it was part of the act.

One girl at the table, Louise, a storyboard artist and filmmaker, fell off her chair, tears streaming down her face. She was completely hysterical with laughter, she couldn't breath. I decided I liked her a lot.

On the third evening, about 2:30 in the morning, after a great pasta salad and coffee cake and wine and a midnight viewing of Being John Malkovich, we started swapping favourite children's television programmes, and golden memories of dreadful shows like Randall and Hopkirk and The Champions - a very common conversation I think. Strange how often these shared memories come up.

There was a pause. There were only four of us still up, the house was silent, the night was dark dark blue, a slight smell of fried onions and garlic from the kitchen.

Louise looked at me and said, "I remember being able to fly".

"Yes," I said.

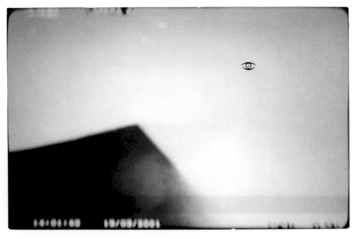

these stories written over ten year period

yet the themes remain the same

reaching back to childhood superman games

reaching forward to my hopes for the next thing

whatever it is

i'm sure it will fly

[i make these thoughts into tangible objects

and drain them of their potential energy]

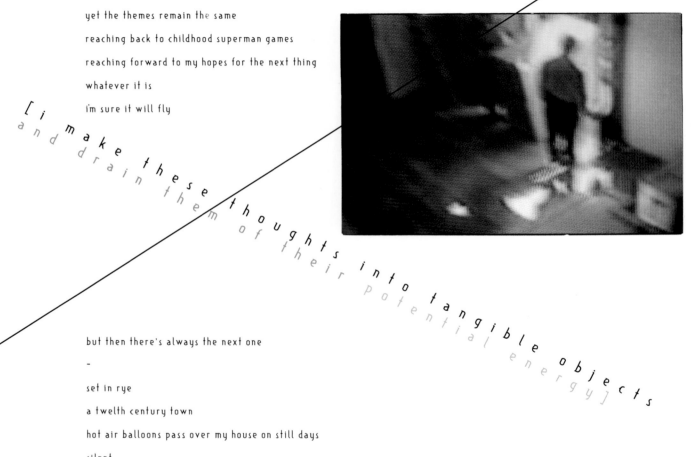

but then there's always the next one

-

set in rye

a twelfth century town

hot air balloons pass over my house on still days

silent

you can hear their conversation

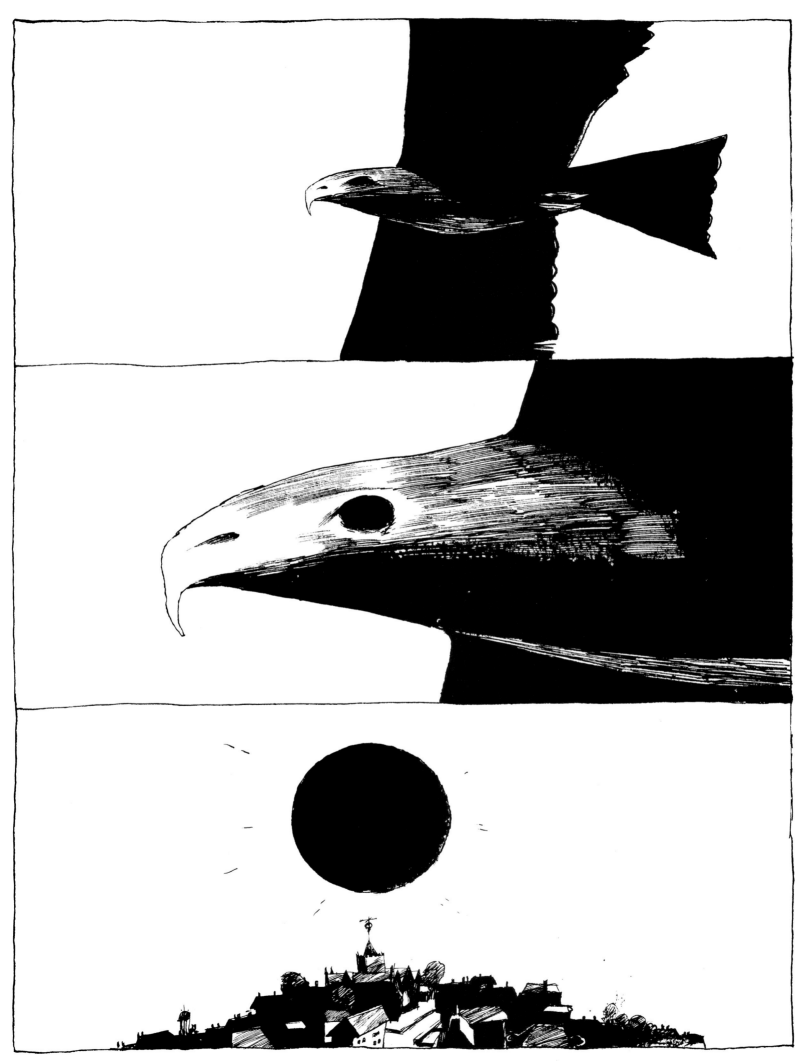

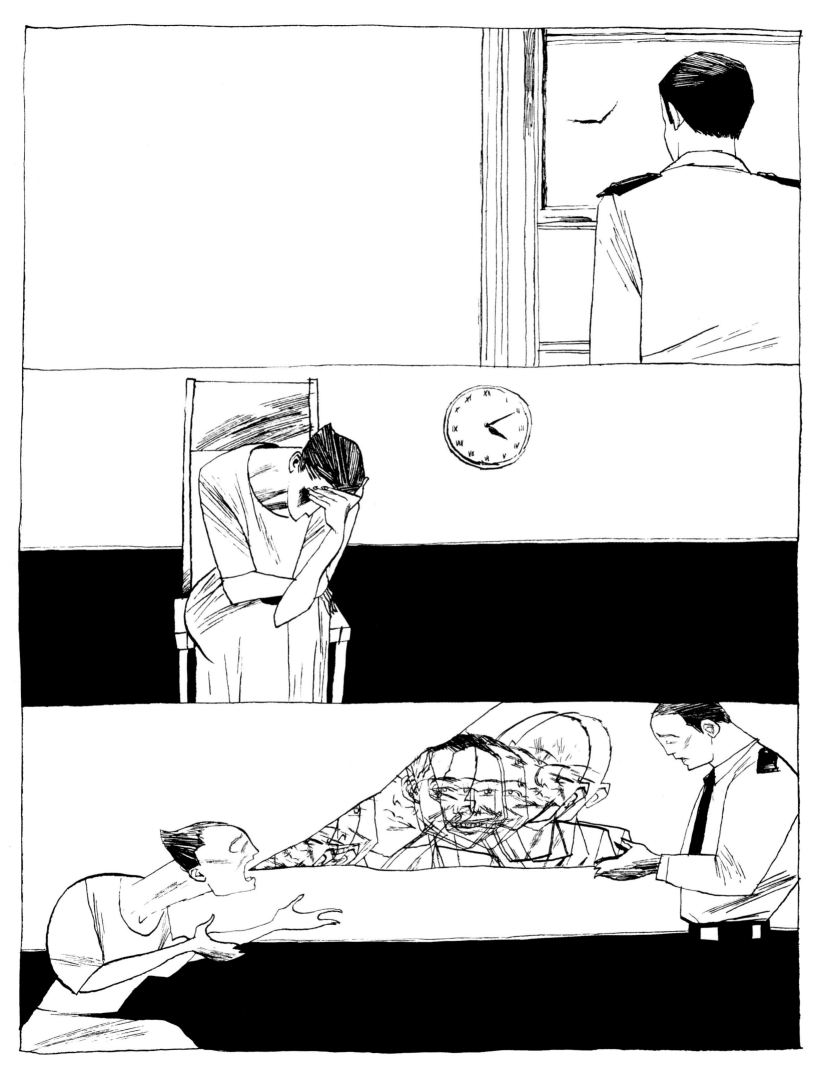

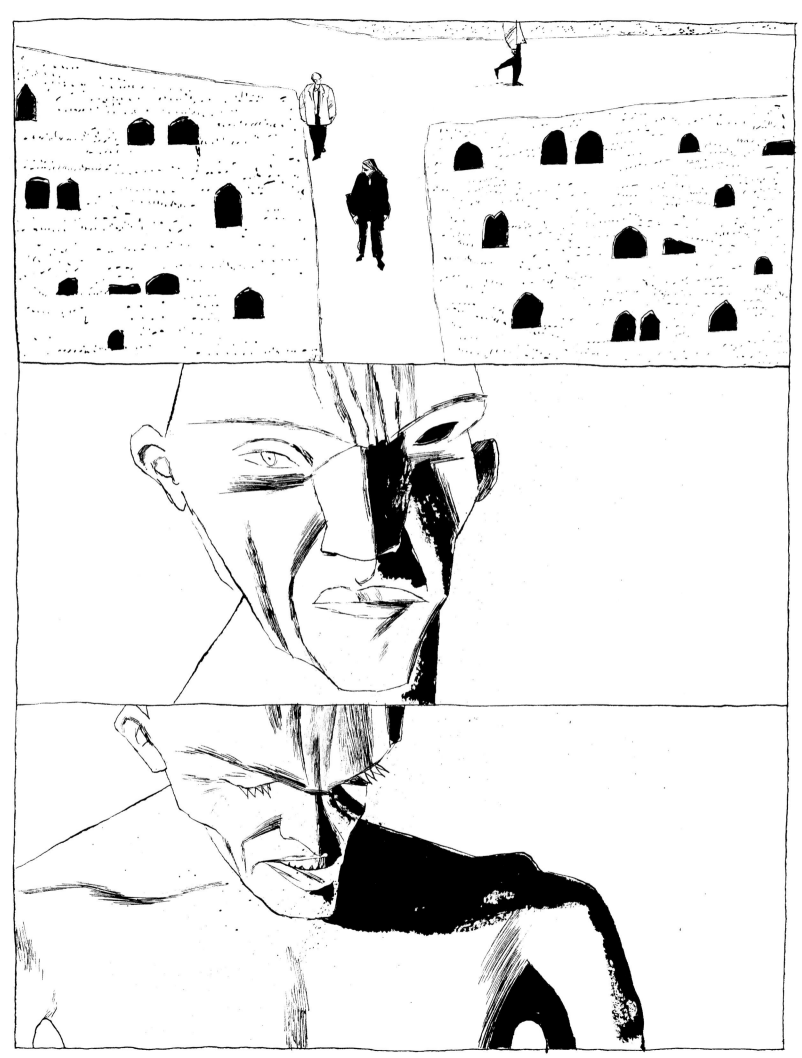

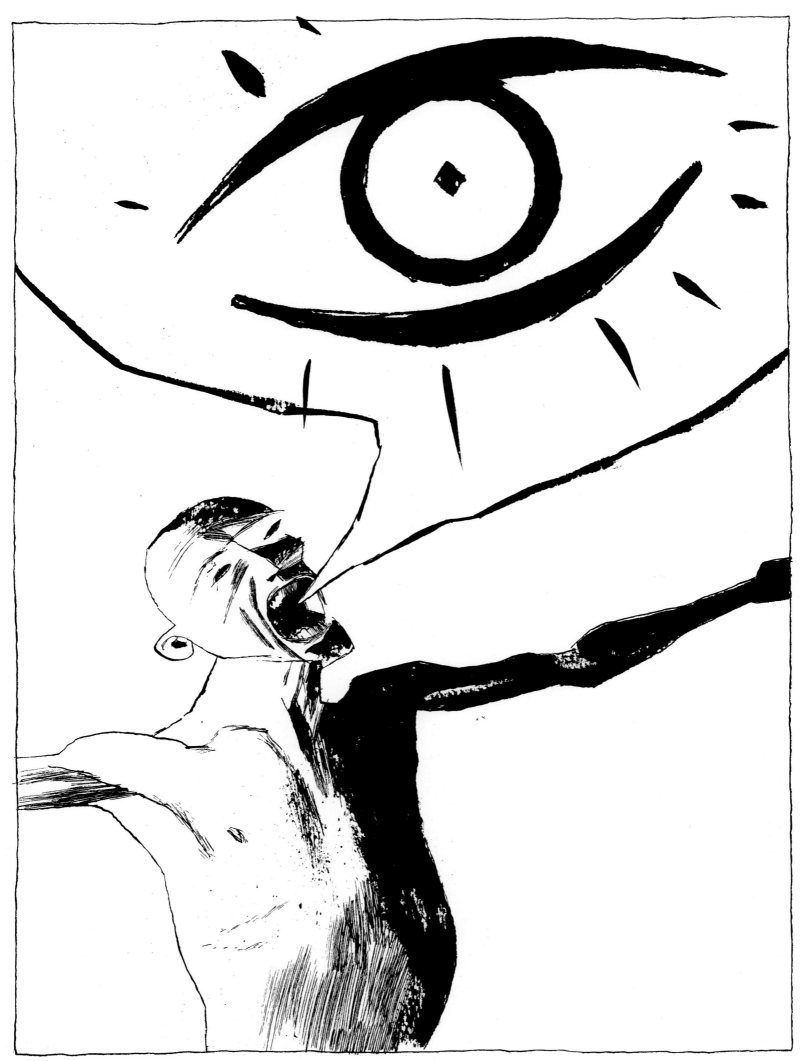

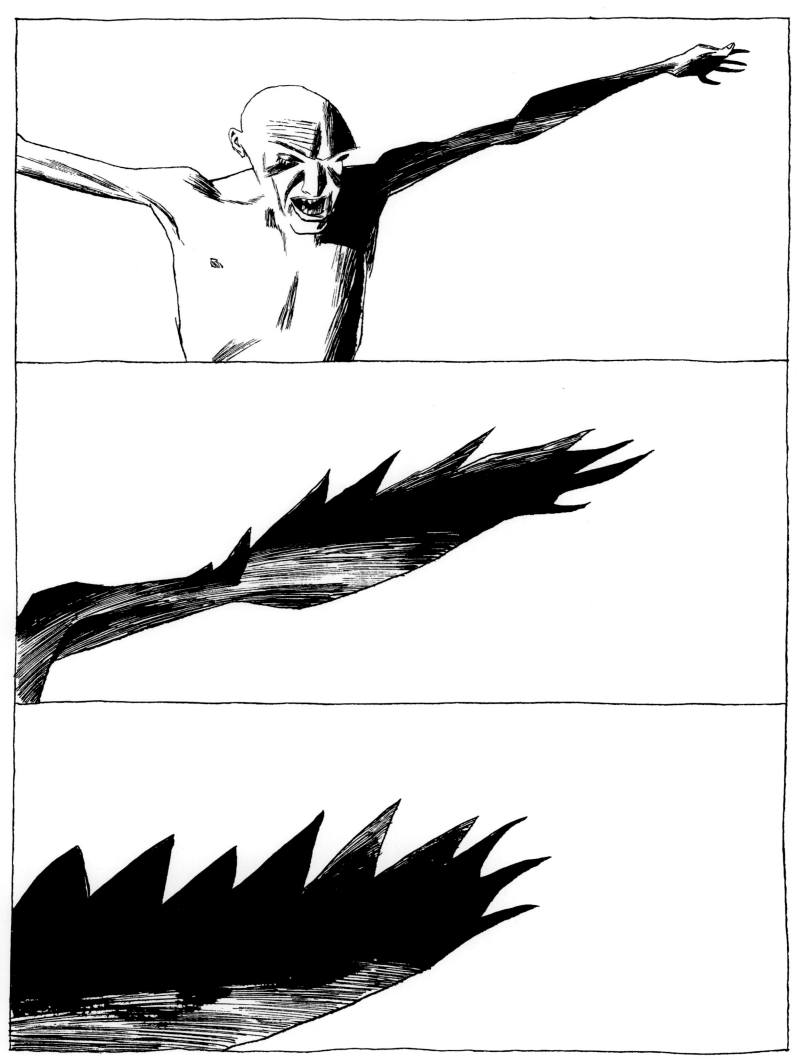

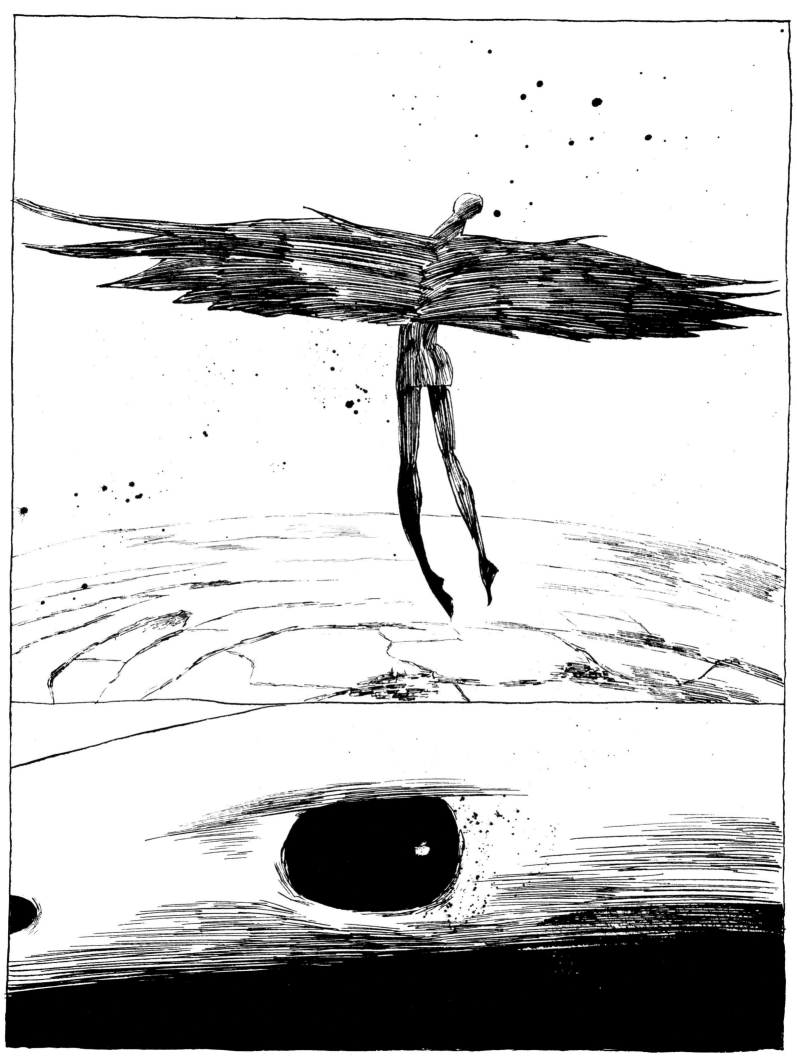

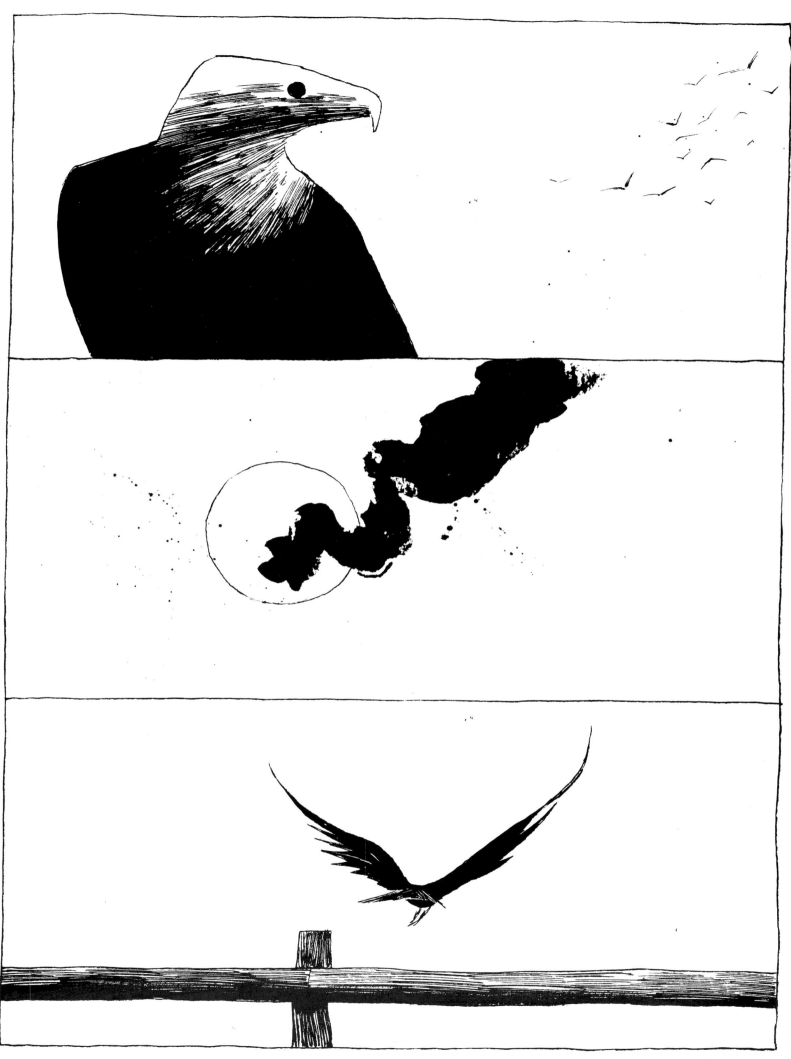

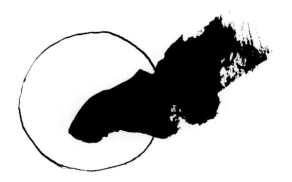

bitten & bruised

a persistent dream

lying next to my wife

lifting the covers while she sleeps

afraid of what i might see

-        story made for bedateca museum [lisbon]

        fifth anniversary

        exhibition in nineteen ninety eight

        insane band played at opening [vitriol]

        wonderful funny scary sounds

        pickups on the floor

        cello samples tiny mechanical music boxes

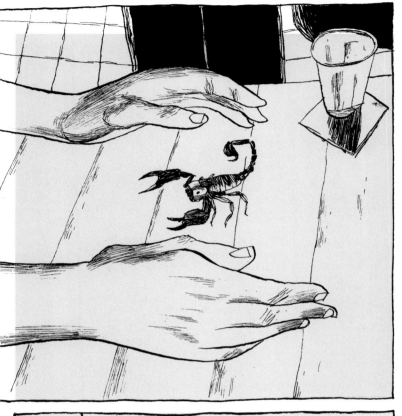

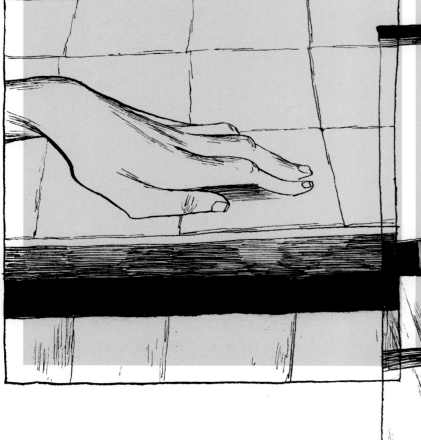

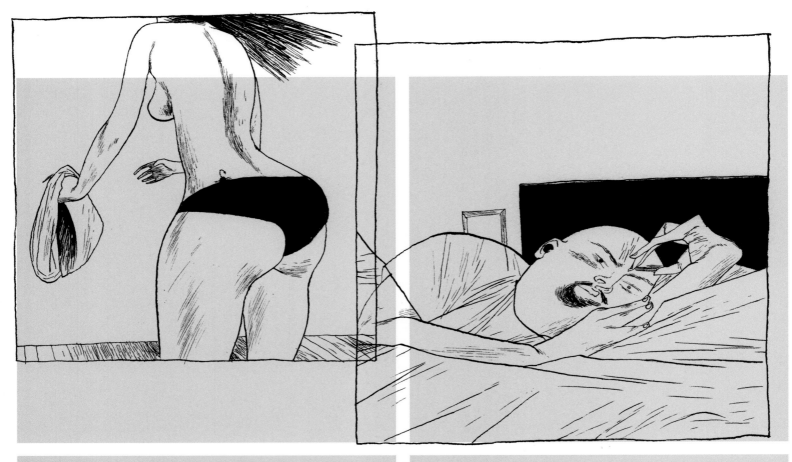
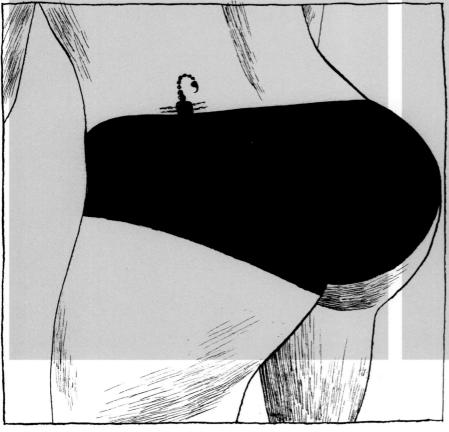

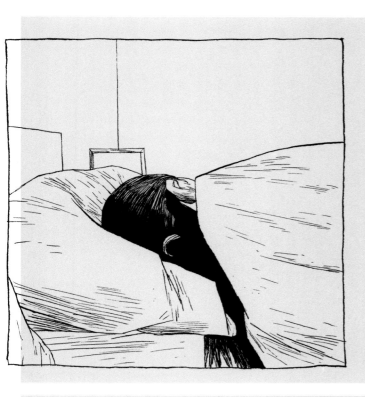

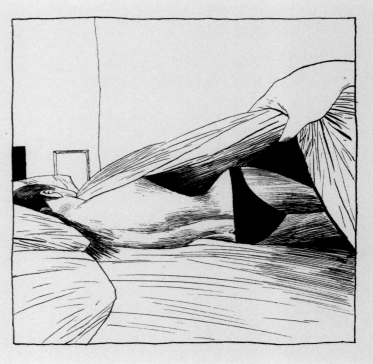

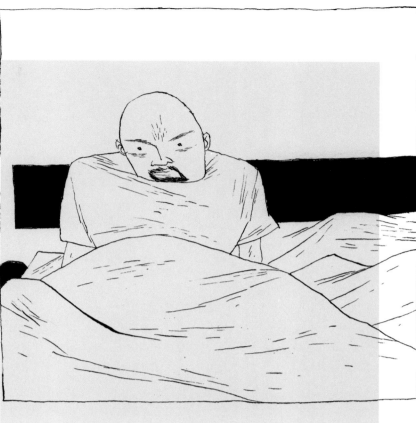

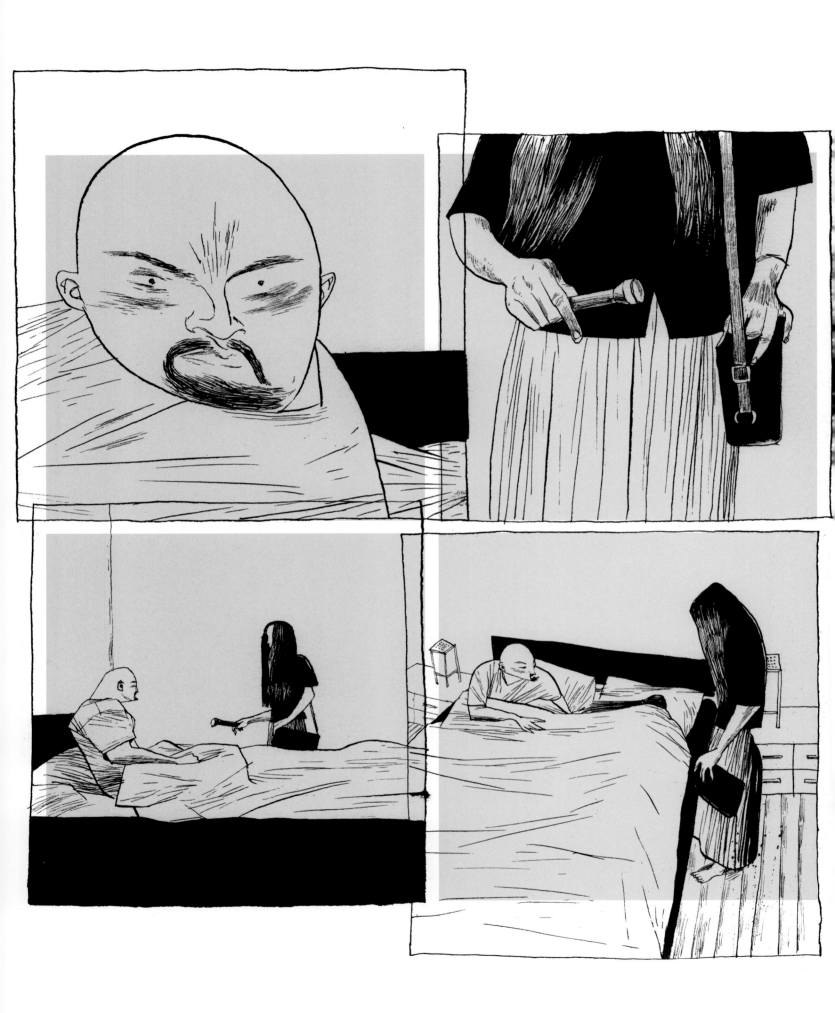

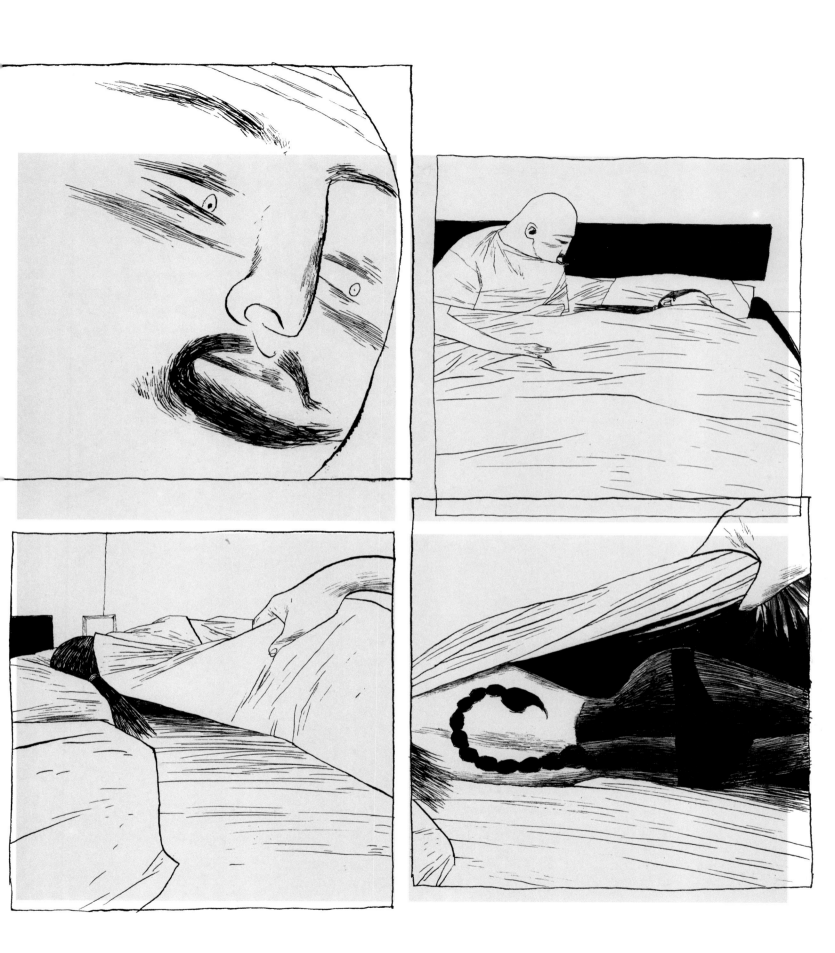

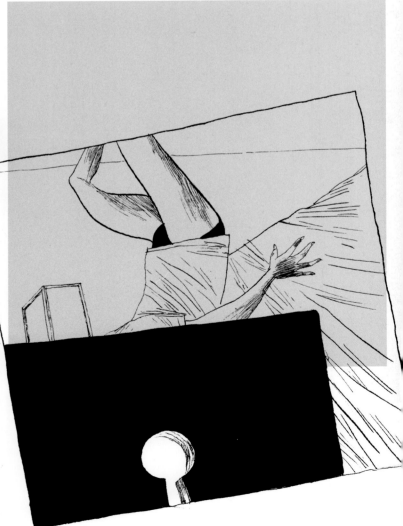

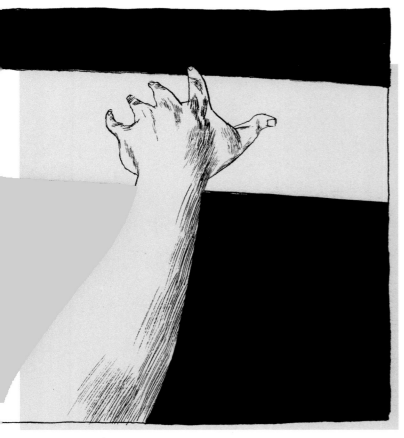

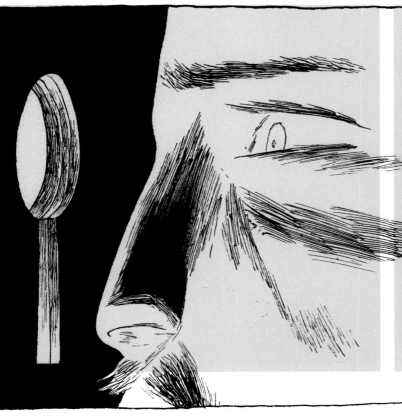

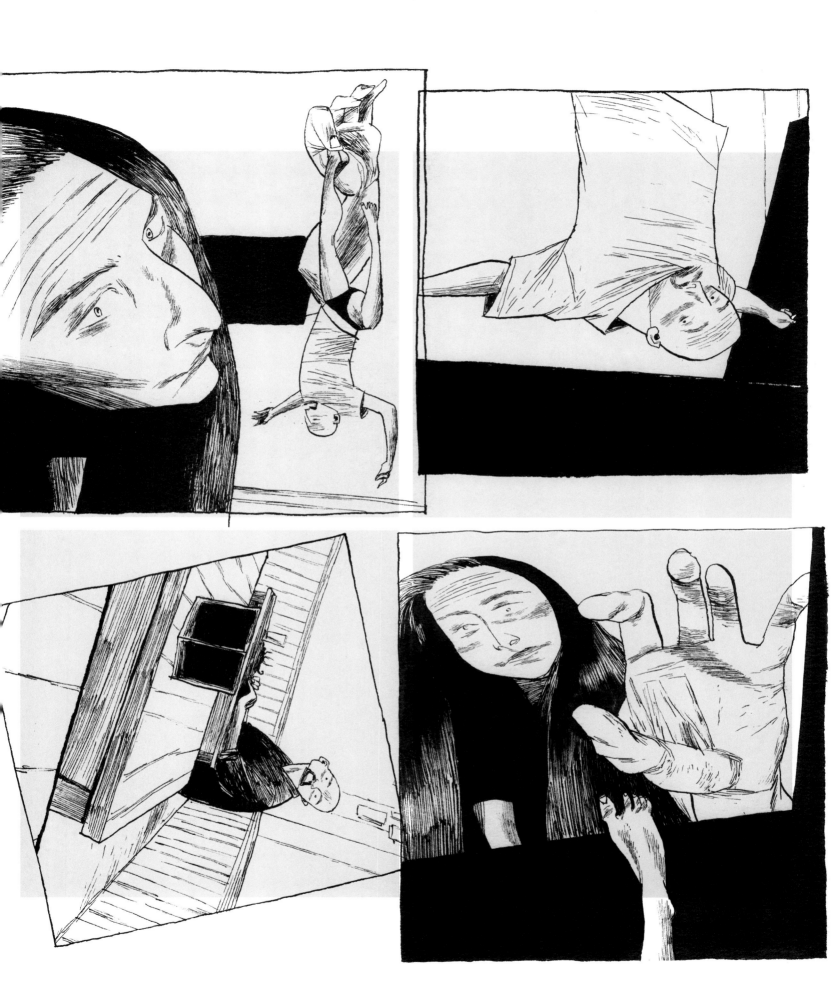

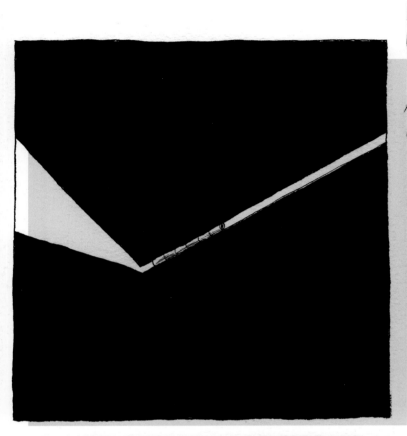
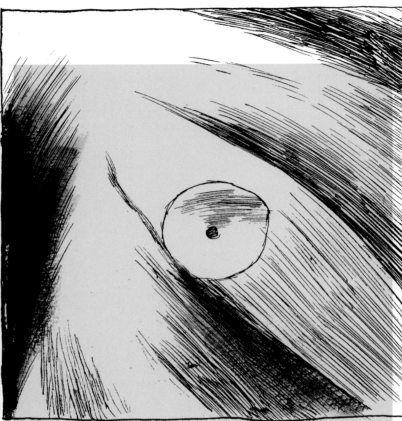
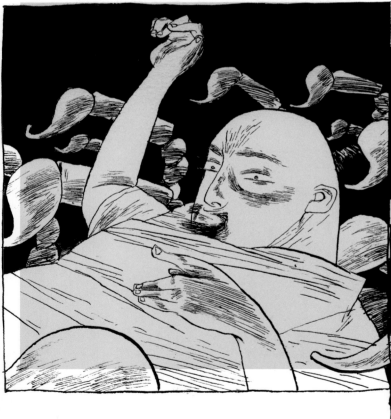

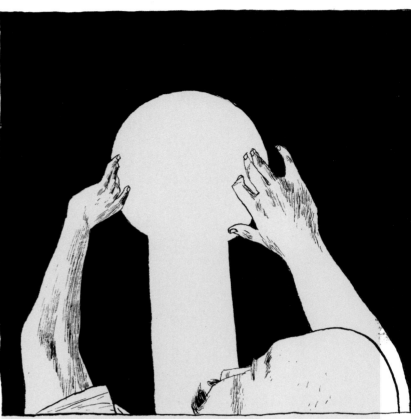

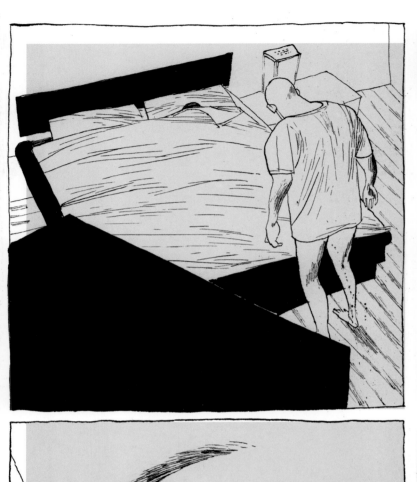

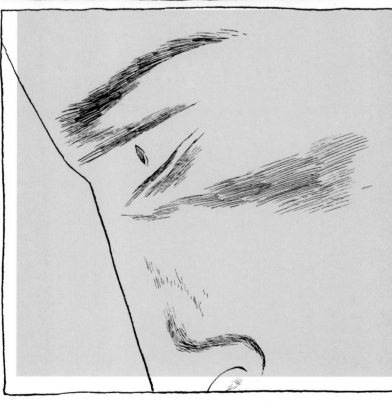

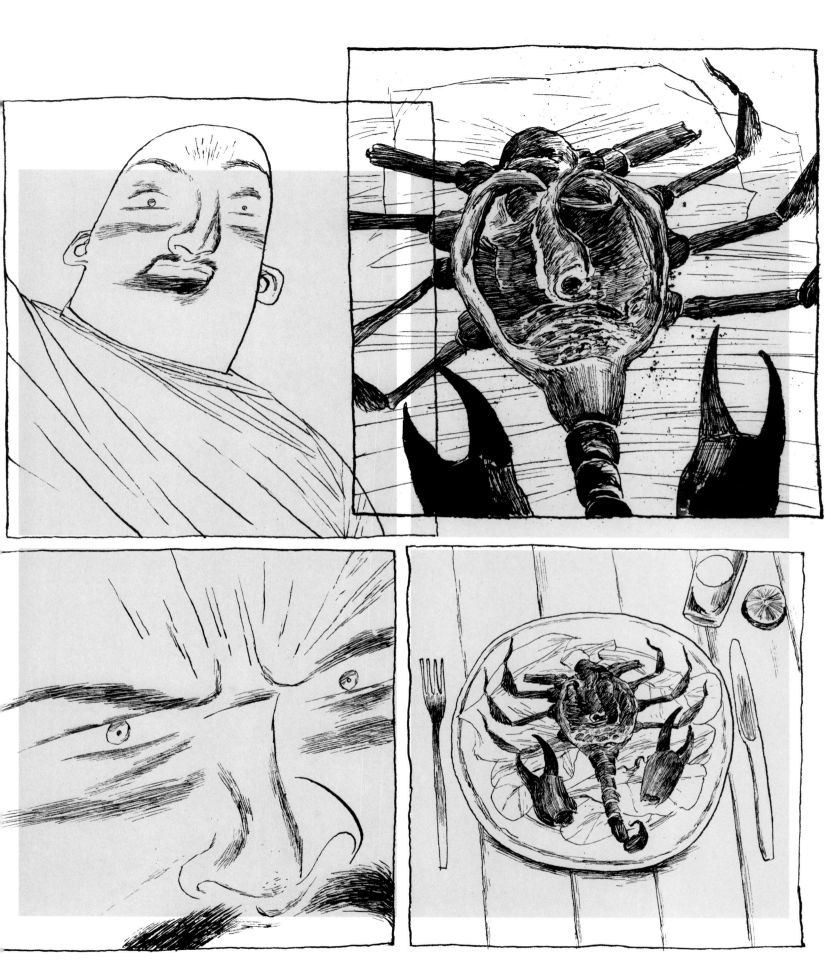

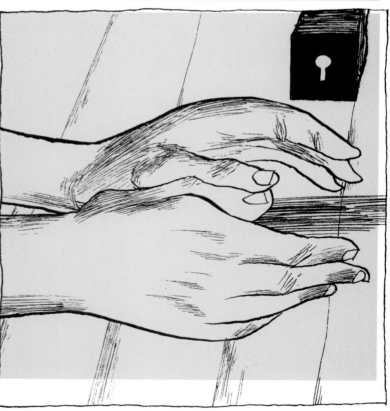

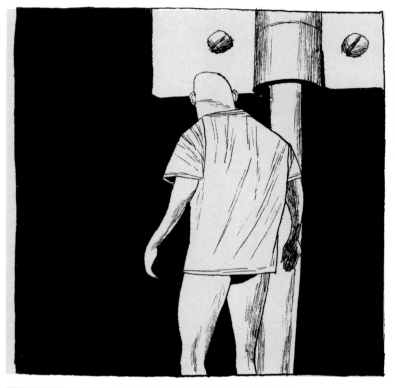

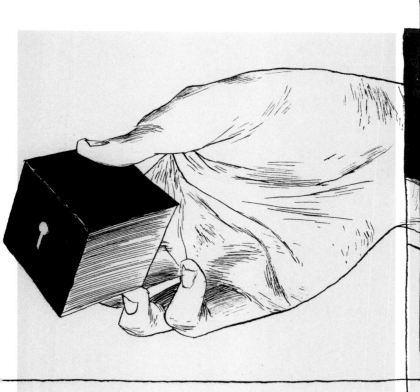

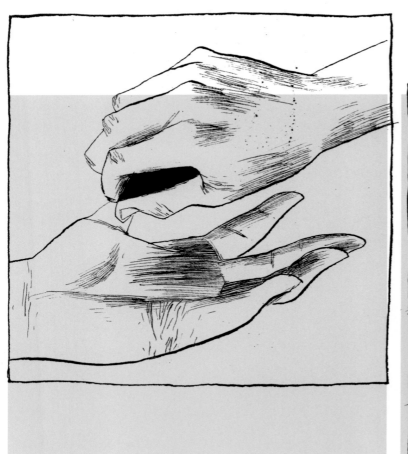
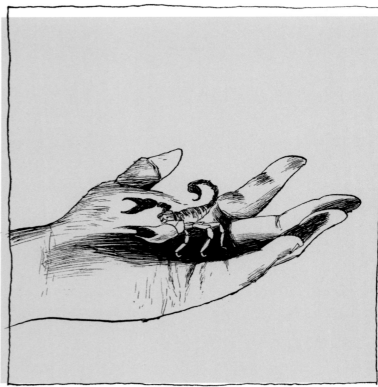

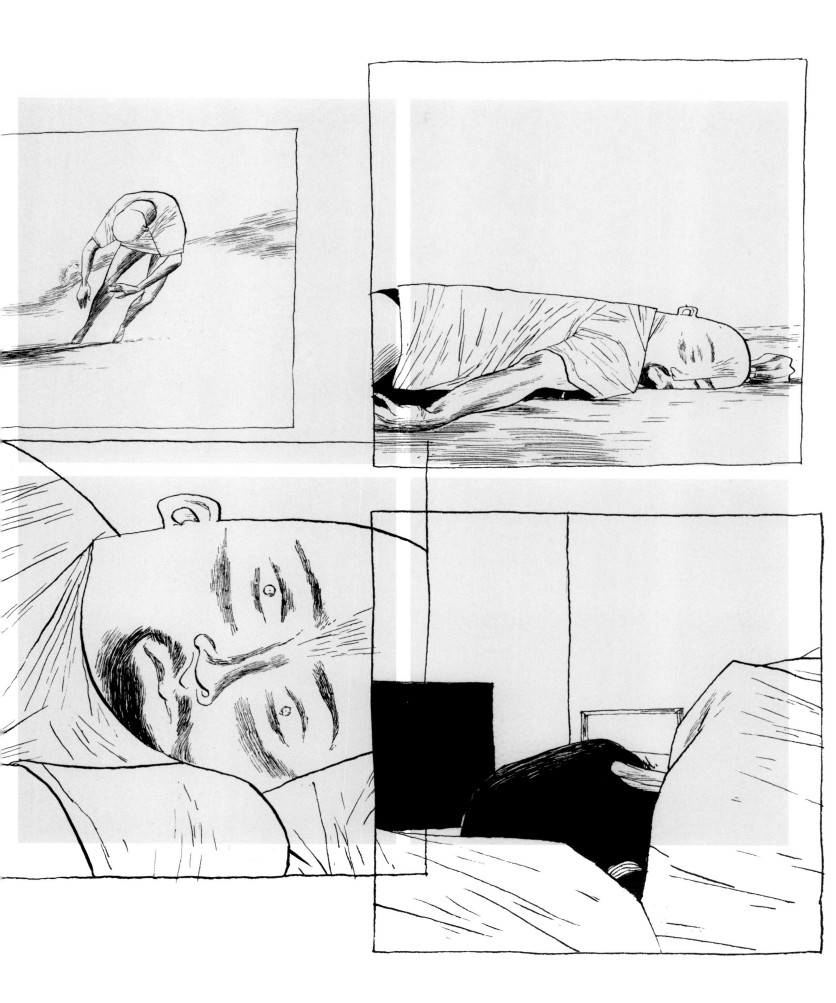

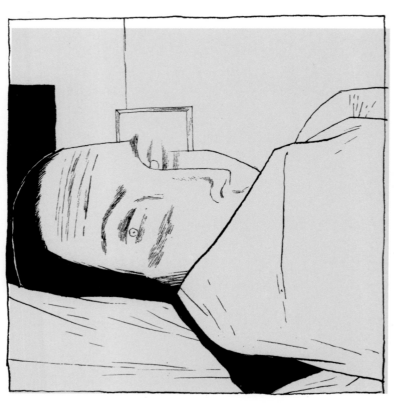
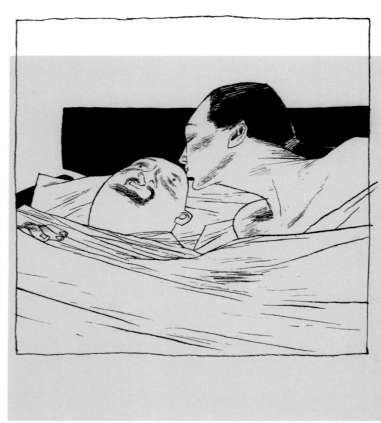

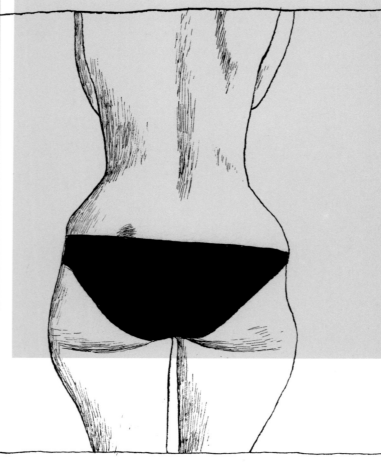

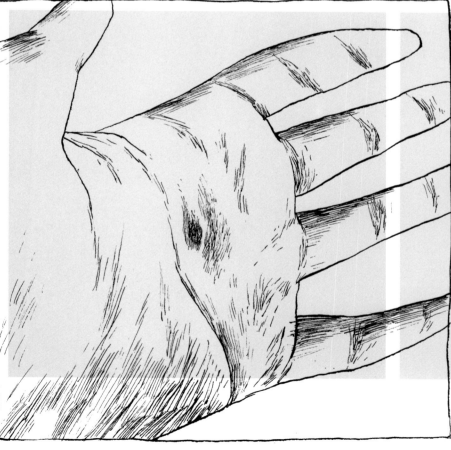

your clothes are dead

accumulation

process

development

chemistry

soil

erosion

-

narrative skitters over the surface

making slight indentations

in a friends life

[fictional]

-

what?

you want sense?

i'm too busy throwing the artwork into the river

to make sense

Your clothes are dead

I have to say I felt low.
Wherever you are, you do the best you can, place one foot in front of the next, your skin is numb,
your eyes fall open, your clothes are dead.

After the funeral and the reception and all those low words.

People came to the house.
They trod on the wooden board that squeaked.
Always managing to hit that board.
I wondered why they never missed that squeaky step, and why that sounds so familiar to me.

I found the paragraph, a book I haven't read for twenty years, IN WATERMELON SUGAR by
Richard Brautigan. The squeaky step bit. A feeling that tilts the floor under my feet, reading
something, hearing in my head, something I haven't heard for twenty years, a different life.
The book of his I really loved was THE ABORTION. I borrowed it from a friend when I was twenty?
Twenty-one? I've never been able to find a copy.

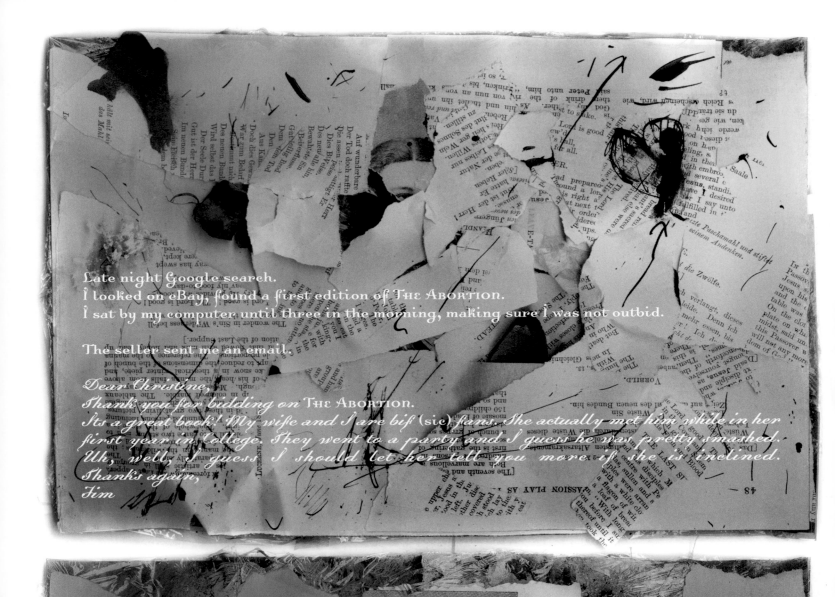

Late night Google search.
I looked on eBay, found a first edition of THE ABORTION.
I sat by my computer until three in the morning, making sure I was not outbid.

The seller sent me an email.

Dear Christine,
Thank you for bidding on THE ABORTION.
Its a great book! My wife and I are bif (sic) fans. She actually met him while in her
first year in College. They went to a party and I guess he was pretty smashed.
Uh, well, I guess I should let her tell you more if she is inclined.
Thanks again,
Jim

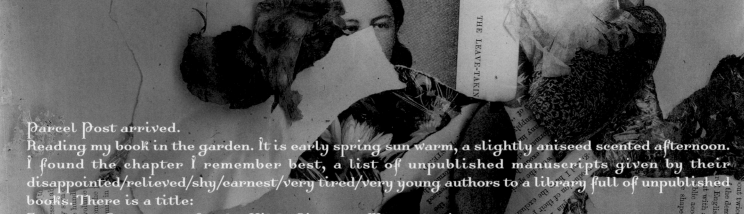

Parcel Post arrived.
Reading my book in the garden. It is early spring sun warm, a slightly aniseed scented afternoon.
I found the chapter I remember best, a list of unpublished manuscripts given by their
disappointed/relieved/shy/earnest/very tired/very young authors to a library full of unpublished
books. There is a title:
JACK, THE STORY OF A CAT by Hilda Simpson. My mother's name.
I sit with this fact, my mother's name famous in front of me.
The peach sun fades. I go back into the house.
I sent an email to Jim, thanking him for sending the book so quickly.
He returned my email acknowledging the thanks and the positive feedback I left for him on
eBay.
More information about his wife and Richard Brautigan was not forthcoming.

I cleared out the remains of my mother's bric-a-brac today.
Hats, pots, threads, piano, bathroom blandities, draft excluders, glasses and books, books, books.
So many books.
The house is sold and cold and silent. It has paid off my mortgage and put my savings so far in
the black I feel crushed by guilt every time I drive past the bank. I have profited by loss.

In the night, the layers of grief seem to fall away. Whether I'm dreaming or lying awake,
listening to the cuckoo.

Last night I heard a rustle, through the hall, in the living room.
I sat up, straining to hear any sound closer than the trees.
I walked silently, slowly out of the bedroom, through the hall. In the doorway I paused, a small
black movement, and then a quiet panic, a rush of shadow, and I think a cat ran out toward the
kitchen.
I ran after it, I don't have a cat flap any more, but the cat was gone. I looked under cupboards,
and any small hiding places I could find. No cat.
As I walked back to my bed I noticed the book was open on the coffee table. Open on the page
headed JACK,...

The internet has become the library from Brautigan's 1970 imagination. Pages and pages of private diaries, collections, lists and photographs, made public in HTML. The need to make your mark, plant your flag. But even Wet Wilbur's Collection of Extracted Facial Hair homepage had been visited 23 times. In the book no-one comes to read or borrow the handwritten or two finger typed stories that stack on the shelves collecting dust and spiderwebs. I looked up Richard Brautigan's various pages, now a small section in his own library. I forgot that he had killed himself at forty nine, like Ernest Hemingway, a single gunshot to the head. Friends still come to my door, squeaking inevitably, knocking cautiously, concerned, giving me cake.

The following night, drinking Merlot, reminding me of California, I thought I heard my night visitor again, paper scuffs, my own dull heart beat.
I crept to the living room door. The cat caught in silhouette against moonlight on the wall, crouched on the table, The Abortion open in front of its nose. It appeared to be reading. I sat in the doorframe, sipped my wine, and stayed with the cat as it slowly read a chapter, turning the pages awkwardly, pushing a paw from right to left, the scuff sound I recognised. Eventually the cat looked up, ears forward, eyes alert, it jumped and skittered into the darkness.

In July I fly to California. Every year I will see friends in San Diego, and then stay for a couple of weeks in Monterey or San Francisco. Over the years San Diego has changed a lot. When I first came there was a mall and a harbour and a sort of war zone in between, walk there at night and get mugged.

But now there is a downtown, a cosmopolitan and vital streetlife. The marzipan soft colours of 50's apartment buildings have been ignited by hot Moroccan splashes and cool spearmint turquoise stucco.

I took Jim the bookseller's business card with me. It had fallen out of the book when I had unpacked it a couple of months ago, landing on my coffee table, a swirly 'with thanks' written on the back.

He was based in Big Sur. I half imagined dropping by.

I drove north along the coast road, avoiding Los Angeles as best I could.

Those dry rolling hills, flat trees, local artichoke festivals.

I emailed Jim from my hotel room. His reply was positive. I wasn't sure what I wanted to find.

I knocked on his door. A Spanish wooden knock, a light violet villa style bungalow, a huge red poppy painted onto the wall, its stems twining around the windows.

The door opened. Jim, looking like Brautigan of course, older, lank blonde hair, droopy moustache, gable eyebrows, said 'hi', gestured me into the front room. There, Jim Simpson and his wife Hilda offered a chair and a drink. My mother seemed to half recognise me, she smiled hello.

No.

The door opened and Jim, who was blonde but did not posses a Brautigan moustache or noticeably gable eyebrows for that matter said 'hi'. His wife was not there.

He made me coffee with cardamon, and we sat amongst the stacks of books and haze of late afternoon. I realised I had found a home for all my mother's books, if he'd like to deal with them.

We talked about the Monterey aquarium and the jellyfish, the pelicans and the ever rising price of local property, we talked about George Dubbelyuh Bush and Annie Robinson, and we didn't talk about his wife.

And finally a pause lasted a couple of beats too long, Jim shuffled his feet and prepared to say *'well...'* and I looked at a photograph by my chair, a young happy hippie couple on the beach, and asked about his wife. Jim had gable eyebrows after all. She had died several years ago, he still talked about her in the present tense, in emails and letters.

We talked long into the night, he seemed to have saved up all of his stories and anecdotes for this one evening. I told him about my mother's singing and her Rogers and Hammerstein medley. We laughed a lot.

At the end of summer, back in England.
Getting over the jet lag for a day or two.
Packing up boxes of books.
I finished reading The Abortion very slowly, waiting for a nod from the cat before turning the page.

When we finished on a fresh, post thunder storm night, he walked toward the front door, I followed. He led me out of the house, down the drive and out onto the pavement. We walked to the edge of the village and cut across to a public footpath, out into the fields, heading I realised toward my mother's house, about five crow fly miles inland.
We arrived and looked into the kitchen window, still empty, sold as a holiday home to wealthy Belgians who didn't appear to need a holiday that year.

The cat led me through the garden, around the side of the house to the regimented flowerbeds at the back. And beyond. Past overgrown mulch pits and conifer hedges to the very farthest corner of the property. A small stone grave marker almost covered in strawy grass. And I remembered. I must only have been about twelve. Our cat Jack died. My mother let me paint a little cat onto a stone marker here now weathered but still visible. She thought I would be too upset to see Jack in the ground, covered with soil, so I stayed in the house with my granny, her mother, as she dug, laid the body and a cloth at her feet, shovelled and cried.

I lifted the stone to one side, pulled the grass away, dug into the dirt. The blue cloth was near the surface. I pulled it out of the soil and a plastic envelope fell to the ground. Inside was a book, my mother's copy of THE ABORTION. My own memories unravelled, had I read this copy twenty years ago, had I borrowed a different book from a friend, did I have a friend? I took the book out of its sealed time capsule and sat on the grass. I remembered the photograph on the front, a young woman looking straight to camera, I remembered the typeface. Inside, on the title page was written;
    'For Hilda, Thank you for your cat story, I hope you don't mind that it sits on a shelf in the library in this book. With love, and luck, Richard'.

Two final entries.

I have started working again, just part-time, writing the odd review, copy editing, living with words.

I bought a kitten, someone said that a house <u>can</u> be a home without a cat in it, but how would it know?

Oh yes, I realise this may sound strange, but I decided to put my mother's copy of THE ABORTION up for auction on eBay. I have my own copy now, that first edition that took me across the world, and led me out of the dark. It turned out to be a rebirth in the end, if that doesn't sound too obvious.

It was rare for Brautigan to sign his books, especially the early ones.

I hoped it would find a new home, maybe the daughter of one of the other authors whose books litter the shelves of the library, maybe one of those very authors. Mr. Charles Green whose book had been rejected 459 times, or Barbara Jones and her book called PANCAKE PRETTY which was about a pancake, a child at the time, she must be thirty eight now? Or maybe just someone feeling low, needing someone or something to take them by the hand, across the room, across the fields, across the page.

lillie little lillie

written for the residents' freak show

lillie is the freak who freaks out the freaks

-

finished just before visiting berlin in
          nineteen ninety four

[snipers picking off tourists]

[shrapnel craters pitting museum walls]

[searching for cabaret dreams]

-

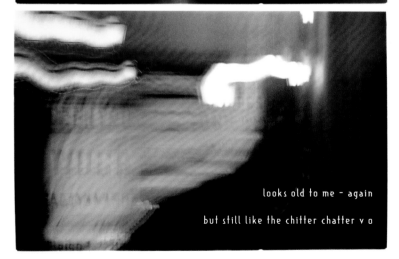

showed the piece to brian bolland

comics artist who introduced me to the residents

he thought it looked like the music

the nicest thing he could have said

-

looks old to me - again

but still like the chitter chatter v o

I JUST TURN AROUND, YOU SEE?

I TURN AROUND JUST LIKE THAT

NOT EVEN A TURN,

JUST A LOOK

A LOOK IN THE WRONG DIRECTION

SO I LOOK AND THERE'S THIS SPACE IN THE CROWD

AND I SAY SHIT, YOU KNOW WHAT'S THIS YOU KNOW THIS SPACE IN THE CROWD

SO I LOOK AGAIN

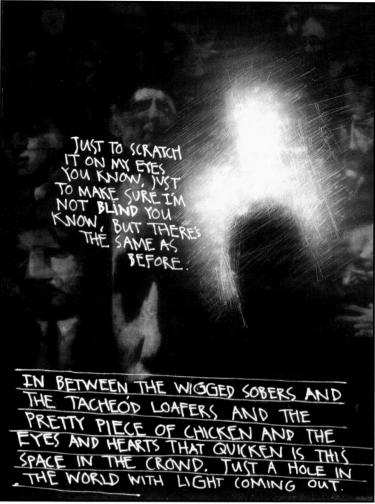

JUST TO SCRATCH IT ON MY EYES YOU KNOW, JUST TO MAKE SURE I'M NOT BLIND YOU KNOW, BUT THERE'S THE SAME AS BEFORE.

IN BETWEEN THE WIGGED SOBERS AND THE TACHE'D LOAFERS AND THE PRETTY PIECE OF CHICKEN AND THE EYES AND HEARTS THAT QUICKEN IS THIS SPACE IN THE CROWD. JUST A HOLE IN THE WORLD WITH LIGHT COMING OUT.

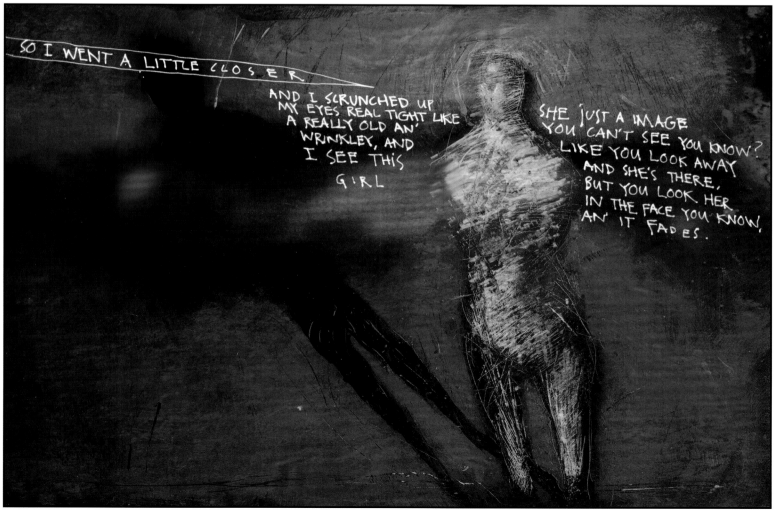

SO I WENT A LITTLE CLOSER

AND I SCRUNCHED UP MY EYES REAL TIGHT LIKE A REALLY OLD AN' WRINKLEY, AND I SEE THIS

GIRL

SHE JUST A IMAGE YOU CAN'T SEE YOU KNOW? LIKE YOU LOOK AWAY AND SHE'S THERE, BUT YOU LOOK HER IN THE FACE YOU KNOW, AN' IT FADES.

NOT LIKE THAT GUY,
REMEMBER THAT GUY?
TRYING TO CATCH HIS SHADOW,
OH YEAH HE LIKED THAT,
TRYING TO CATCH THE SPACE
IN THE PALM OF HIS
HANDY WANDY,
LIKE IT WAS A
BUTTERFLY OR SOMETHING

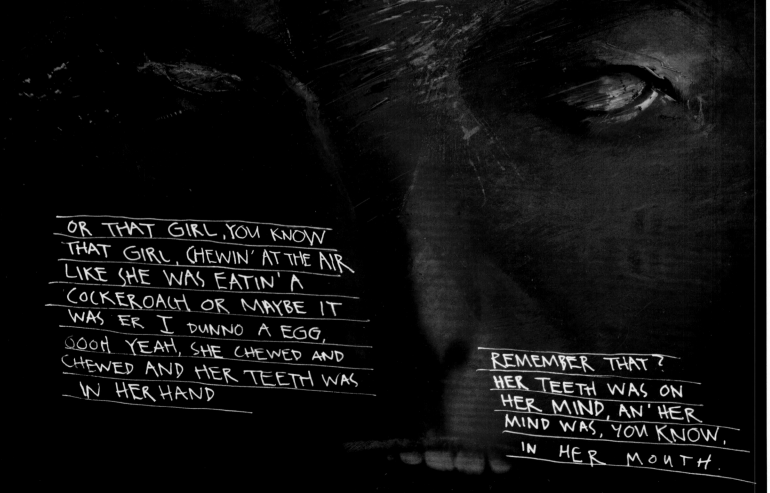

OR THAT GIRL, YOU KNOW
THAT GIRL, CHEWIN' AT THE AIR
LIKE SHE WAS EATIN' A
COCKEROACH OR MAYBE IT
WAS ER I DUNNO A EGG,
OOOH YEAH, SHE CHEWED AND
CHEWED AND HER TEETH WAS
IN HER HAND

REMEMBER THAT?
HER TEETH WAS ON
HER MIND, AN' HER
MIND WAS, YOU KNOW,
IN HER MOUTH.

BUT THIS IVORY GIRL

THIS CHALK-FACE, SILK
LACE, MILK WHITE STARING
THROUGH ME, YOU KNOW

MAKING DANK COLD PATCHES
OF MILKY SWEAT AT THE
NAPE OF ME.

YOU KNOW?

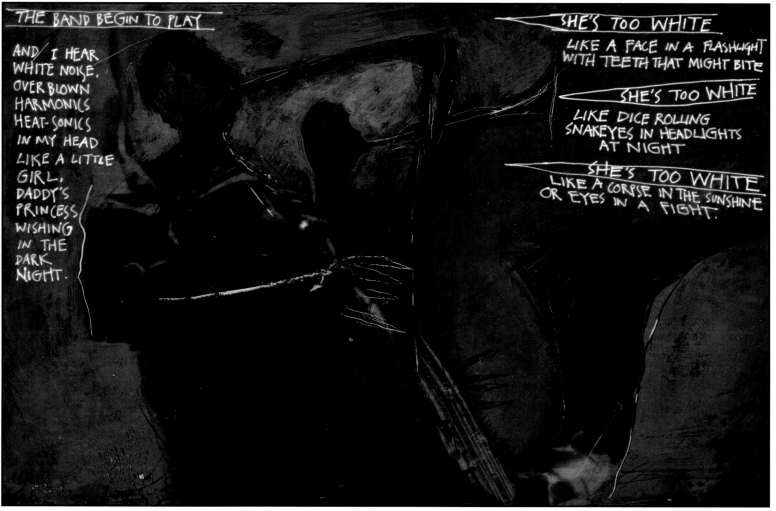

THE BAND BEGIN TO PLAY

AND I HEAR
WHITE NOISE,
OVER BLOWN
HARMONICS
HEAT-SONICS
IN MY HEAD
LIKE A LITTLE
GIRL,
DADDY'S
PRINCESS
WISHING
IN THE
DARK
NIGHT.

SHE'S TOO WHITE
LIKE A FACE IN A FLASHLIGHT
WITH TEETH THAT MIGHT BITE

SHE'S TOO WHITE
LIKE DICE ROLLING
SNAKEYES IN HEADLIGHTS
AT NIGHT

SHE'S TOO WHITE
LIKE A CORPSE IN THE SUNSHINE
OR EYES IN A FIGHT.

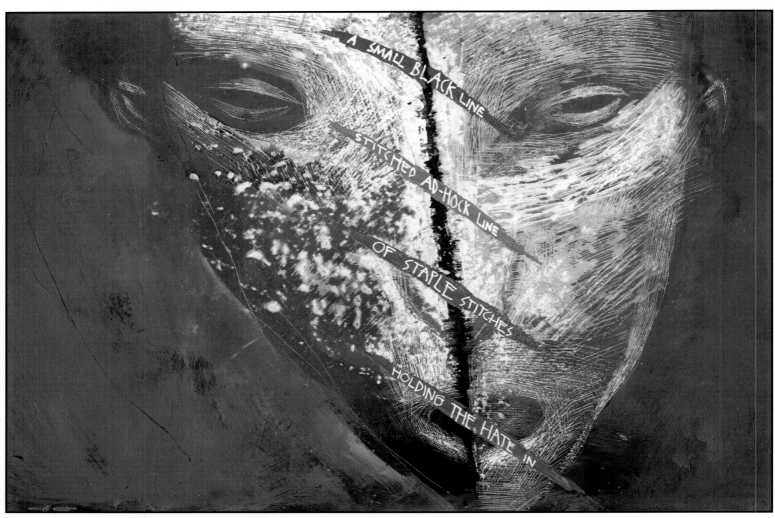

A SMALL BLACK LINE
STITCHED AD-HOCK LINE
OF STAPLE STITCHES
HOLDING THE HATE IN

PULL A THREAD
AND WATCH THE WHOLE FUCKER UNRAVEL
DOMINO TEARS
FALLING HOT, CAUTERISE THE WOUNDS

HATE
DADDY'S
HATE
LITTLE
HATE
PRINCESS

IS THAT ANOTHER SPACE

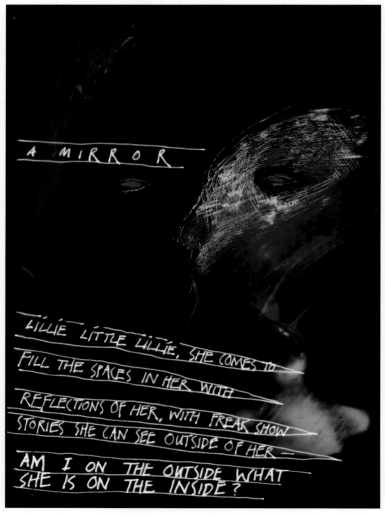

A MIRROR

LILLIE LITTLE LILLIE, SHE COMES TO
FILL THE SPACES IN HER WITH
REFLECTIONS OF HER, WITH FREAK SHOW
STORIES SHE CAN SEE OUTSIDE OF HER —
AM I ON THE OUTSIDE WHAT
SHE IS ON THE INSIDE?

SHIT, I NEED A DRINK.

DAVE McKEAN 10-12-91

the truth is spoken here

piano lessons at eight

bored

studied with jazz pianist at eleven

discovered herbie hancock chick corea joe zawinul

and then the rest

only recently listened properly to art tatum

bloody hell

-

this is an old piece

structured like a standard

theme - solos - restatement of theme

touched up a bit after initial outing in a-one

-

clearly inspired by miles davis

only saw him once

the man with the horn tour

keith jarrett quote -

miles would rather be

making horrible music with

a horrible band than be

doing something he's done

before

this restless irritable dissatisfied drive -

my constant inspiration

The theme is stated

Honestly and with authority

Notes arranged to resonate

To initiate a dialogue

The theme is stated

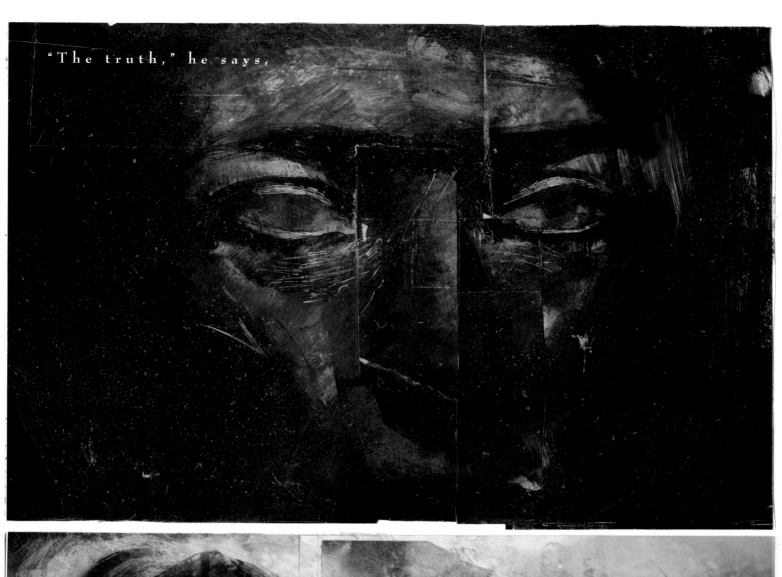

"The truth," he says,

"The truth is spoken here."

CHINESE WHISPERS

One time when Miles wanted to improvise around one repeating chord figure, Herbie said, "You know, I... I like to improvise and everything, but I don't know what to play." And Miles said, "If you don't want to play, don't play."

"Only say something when you have something to say."

THE BURGLAR

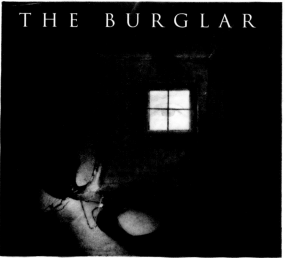

The burglar is a mythological jazz figure in slow swing time.
He tip-toes pizzicato bass lines - he is very clever.

He plucks the drum rhythm out of the air.
His understanding is studied and exacting.

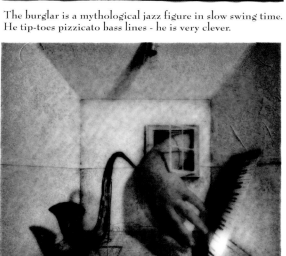

He also lifts the melody. He is the foundation of chords.
He pockets the piano's tuned precision.

With portamento fingers he pilfers the
subtle range of shades between notes.

He counterpoints them all,
and steals away,
hiding behind his shadow.

The Ruler has to draw on all his varied resources when he is called to act for the cause of human happiness.

Play a note. Make a shoe. Grow a tree. Mend a car. Make this activity your own.

These phosphor-dot faces are not real.
Edited and subjectified by the programmers behind the scenery.
Use it, but don't let it use you.

Pride in what and who you are is a strong foundation
But don't be defined by your oppression
Use your anger, don't let it use you.

"Keep control up here," he says.
This is the only tool you need,
They know its power and try to
make it work against you,

Use your mind,
don't let your mind use you.

BLUE CAT

The theme returns,

informed by the experience

of late night conversation.

These lessons need to be passed on.

Blue Cat is curious.

The Uptown Ruler restates the theme.

"The truth,"

he whispers...

DAVE MCKEAN 25/10/92

'THE UPTOWN RULER' IS A MYTHICAL HERO

FROM NEW ORLEANS.

'THE UPTOWN RULER' IS THE 2ND. IN THE BLUES

CYCLE OF RECORDINGS BY WYNTON MARSALIS.

dawn

trying to capture that illusive half seen quality of dreams

small occurrences accumulate significance

locations blur

day for night

reason falls away

thank you duane michals

Dawn

Had it been a real cry colouring her dreams, or a dream cry waking her up.

She thought it had come from the wardrobe.

She watched her own reflection open the door

and offer herself a small cloth bag.

There were drawings on the bag, directions, topographic markings.

She didn't want to follow the map without knowing where it would lead, or how she would get home.

Inside the bag were some glass marbles. They glistened in the moonlight.

She laid each marble on the ground, one at a time, trying to follow the map, a few paces between each marker,

a glistening trail across the bedroom
and out of the door.

Across the brick path and out into the field.

Across the beach and through the kelp pools.

Over the water and around the river banks.

On a tree stump, she stopped and rested, and played games with the marbles.

And then she continued to follow the map across wood,

and frost,

and sand.

Lying amongst the reeds,
she looked at the stars
through the rippling glass
of the marbles.

She looked back at the
little glistening lights,
starry cats eyes,
marking her footsteps.

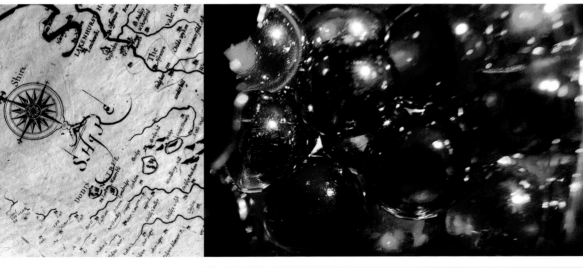

She looked into the cloth bag
with the map sewn into it.
Even though she had travelled a long way,
there were still many marbles left.

She picked up a few of the marbles from her
path and put them back into the bag.

It didn't seem to be any heavier.
It didn't seem to fill up.

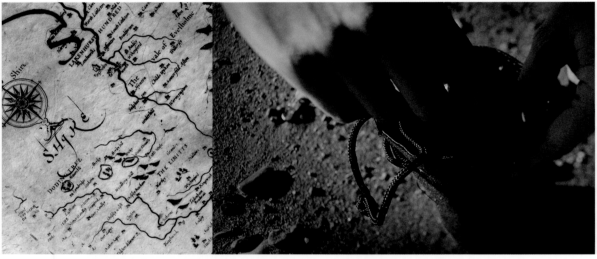

She picked up more marbles and
dropped them into the bag.
She watched them jostle for position,
and yet there was always more room.

She picked up more and more marbles.

And then she realised she had followed the
trail back to her bedroom.

The wardrobe was full of clothes.

It was dawn.

She watched the sun rise and the mist clear over the orchard.

She did the washing up from the previous night and made herself some breakfast.

She planned out some lessons for her class, thought about going to see a movie in the evening.

And she barely noticed the bag of marbles, which she kept safely tucked in her pocket,

just in case she ever needed to escape again.

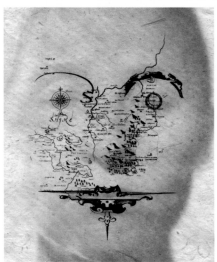

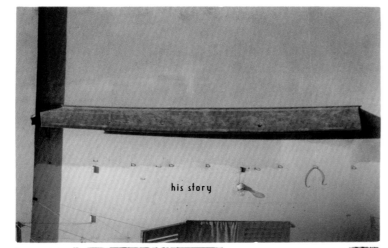

central image noted ten years ago

story hung around

couldn't find a voice

-

his story

reading lots of children's books

brevity of language

concentration of events

-

a life spent trying to look beyond
[while still paying the bills]

acrylic photography and mac

commissioned by kent williams

for bento

story art box

funny name

When I was very young, my father told me his story.

HIS STORY
BY DAVE MCKEAN

It was hard and sharp.
It was cold and smooth.
And clear.
I couldn't really see it.
Just the sharp edges which
I tried not to touch.

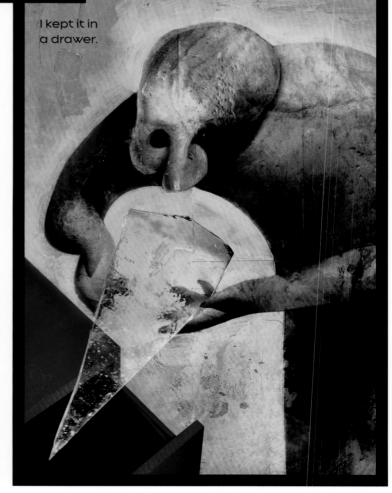

I kept it in
a drawer.

When I was still very young, my father died.

I had not looked at his story
for a few years, so I took it
out of the drawer and
laid it on my bed.
I remembered how
clear it was.
And sharp.
And smooth.

One of the sharp
edges cut my hand.
I washed the blood
away, wrapped his
story in a
handkerchief,

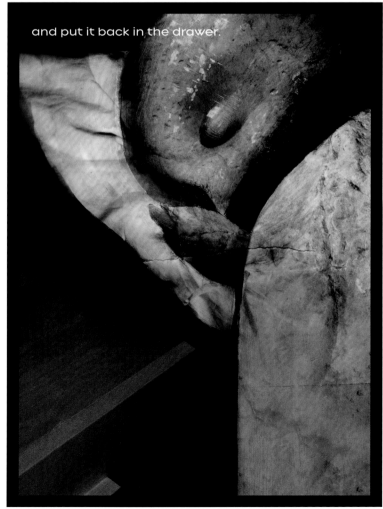

and put it back in the drawer.

When I went to study, I thought I had stopped being very young. In fact, I was even younger. I studied everything I could find. I studied books and people.

I studied fish and aeroplanes. I studied the weather and my mother.

And my father, and one day I decided to study his story.

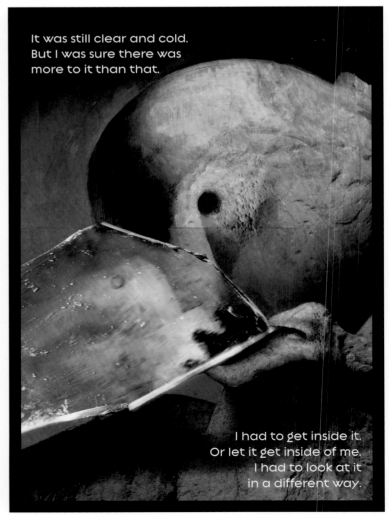

It was still clear and cold. But I was sure there was more to it than that.

I had to get inside it.
Or let it get inside of me.
I had to look at it
in a different way.

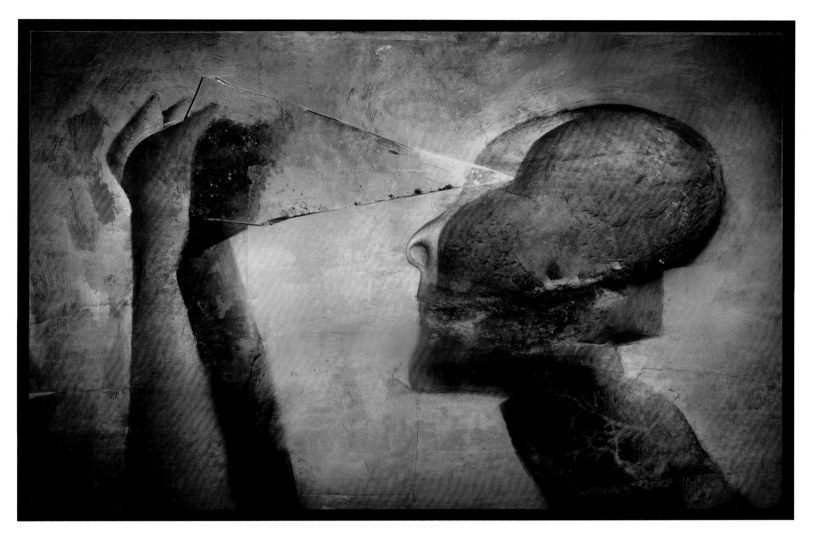

Later, I thought I had made a mistake. There was some pain. And the way I saw everything seemed to have changed. But I had taken an important step. I could not go back now.

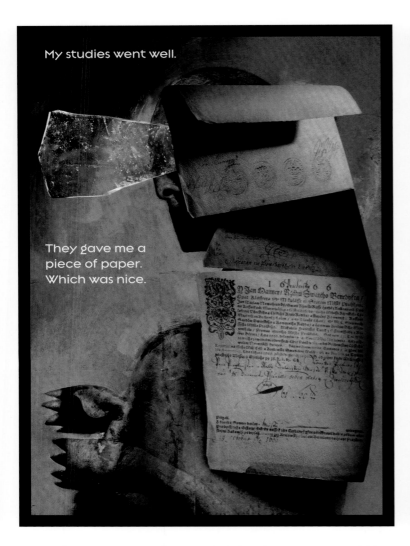

My studies went well.

They gave me a piece of paper. Which was nice.

But the things I had started to see through his story seemed much more important to me.

Everything seemed full of light.
And the light vibrated between violet and red.
I could see the separate pieces of colour that made up everything.
Everything.
It was very exciting.

When I was studying I had forgotten about my age. But I remembered just how young I was when I left home.

Of course I took his story with me, and packed everything else into a crate, with all my books and fish and aeroplanes.

I bought a small tall house. I fell in love.

I started working hard to pay for the house. Lots of things changed in my life, and all of them I watched, reflected in his story.

People told me I was still very young, when I started to think that I might not be. I had a wife and children. I had lots more fish and many more books. I gave my aeroplanes to my children, so most of them were broken.

And I realised that when I looked through his story, I saw a distorted version of the world. A refraction.

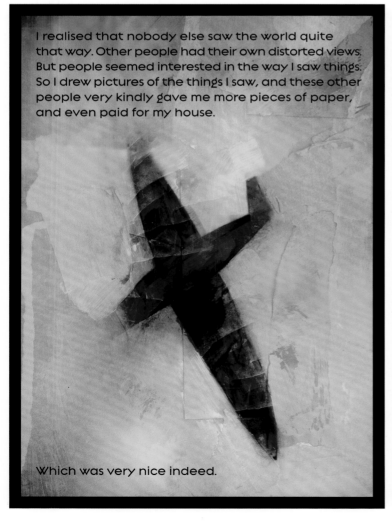

I realised that nobody else saw the world quite that way. Other people had their own distorted views. But people seemed interested in the way I saw things. So I drew pictures of the things I saw, and these other people very kindly gave me more pieces of paper, and even paid for my house.

Which was very nice indeed.

But something had changed.
Most of his story was deep inside me.
It cut through everything.
It filled my head.

Even though my children were determined to convince me otherwise, I was sure I was still very young, when one morning, I woke up and realised that I was the same age as my father had been when he told me his story. And my son was nearly as old as I had been when I listened to his story.
That was a big shock to me, I can tell you.
I don't think I had any breakfast that morning.
I don't think I drew any pictures that day.

I watched my fish swim.
I watched my children play.
I watched my wife read.
Through my own eyes entirely.

I decided that, if at all possible, I really should try to stay very young forever.

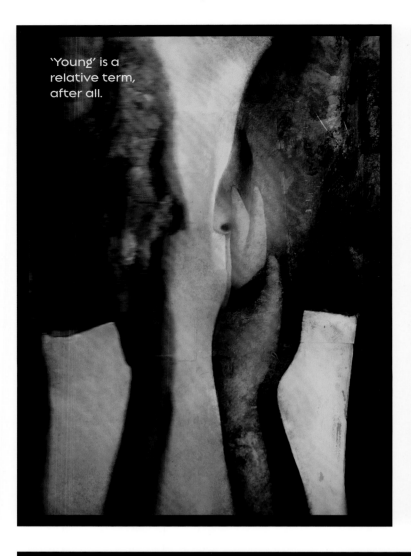

'Young' is a
relative term,
after all.

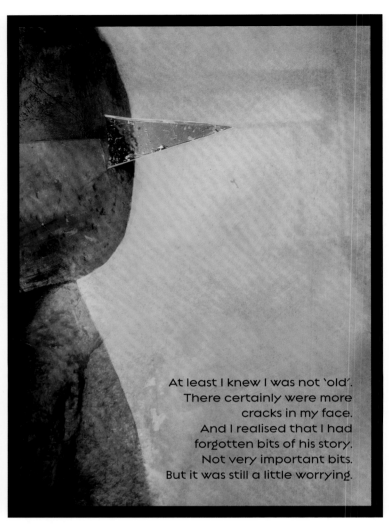

At least I knew I was not 'old'.
There certainly were more
cracks in my face.
And I realised that I had
forgotten bits of his story.
Not very important bits.
But it was still a little worrying.

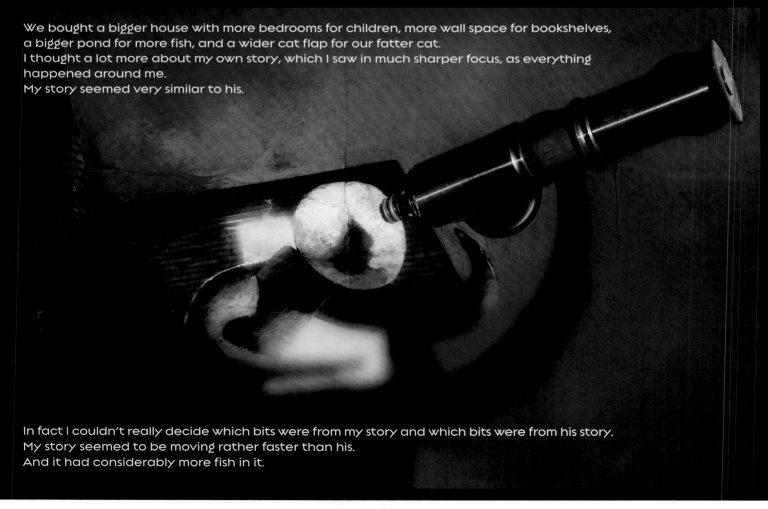

We bought a bigger house with more bedrooms for children, more wall space for bookshelves,
a bigger pond for more fish, and a wider cat flap for our fatter cat.
I thought a lot more about my own story, which I saw in much sharper focus, as everything
happened around me.
My story seemed very similar to his.

In fact I couldn't really decide which bits were from my story and which bits were from his story.
My story seemed to be moving rather faster than his.
And it had considerably more fish in it.

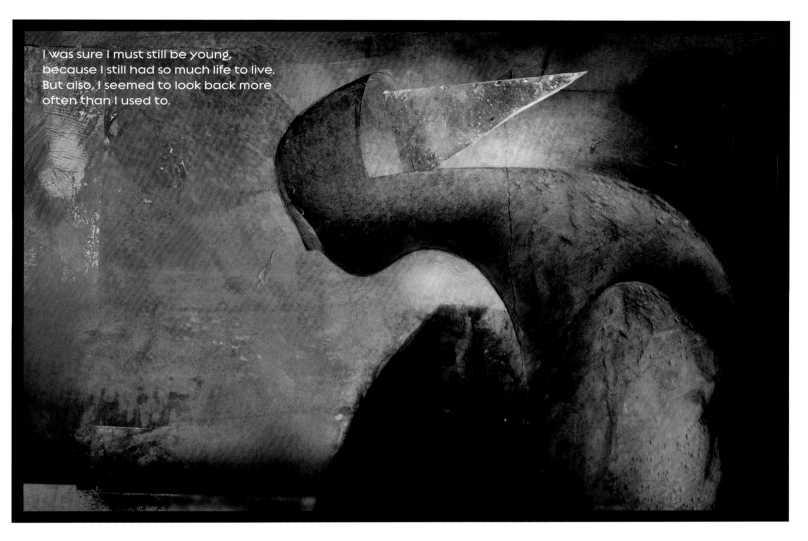

I was sure I must still be young,
because I still had so much life to live.
But also, I seemed to look back more
often than I used to.

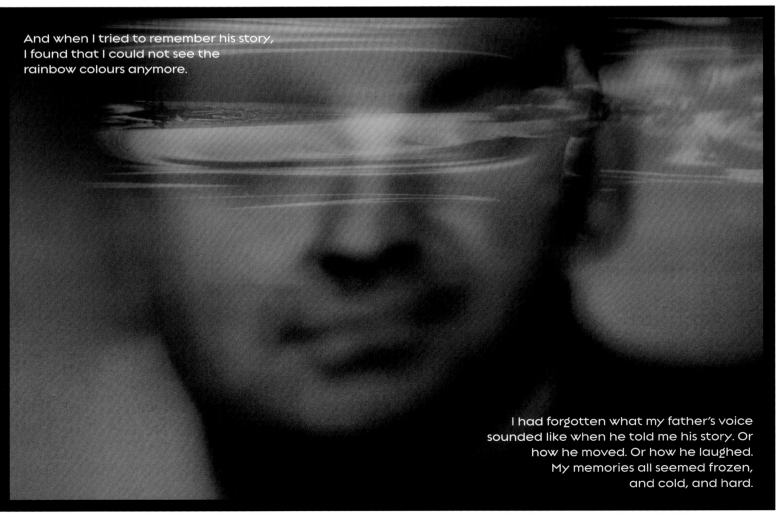

And when I tried to remember his story,
I found that I could not see the
rainbow colours anymore.

I had forgotten what my father's voice
sounded like when he told me his story. Or
how he moved. Or how he laughed.
My memories all seemed frozen,
and cold, and hard.

I am still young.
Certainly people treat me like a child.
Certainly, to me, people seem to behave
more like children.

The days fly by.
The cat dies.
And then the next one dies.
I sleep.
I dream.
I get up.
I move about.
I'm really quite tired.

I did wonder, one day,
if I remembered to tell
my story to my son.
I think I did.
Yes, I'm sure I did.

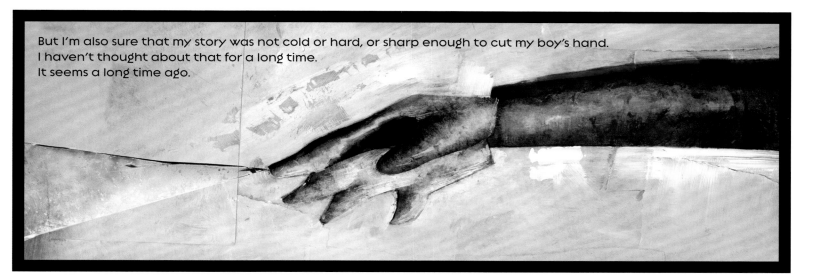

But I'm also sure that my story was not cold or hard, or sharp enough to cut my boy's hand.
I haven't thought about that for a long time.
It seems a long time ago.

In amongst the sleeping and the getting up,

and the moving about...

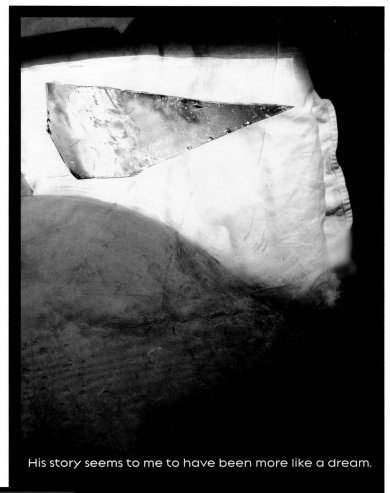

His story seems to me to have been more like a dream.

THE END

DECEMBER 2000

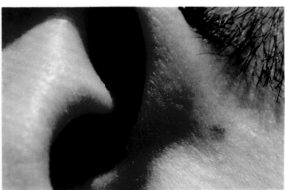

dave mckean was born in england in

1963 and since leaving berkshire college
1982-1986
of art + design has illustrated several

award winning comix
arkham asylum mr punch signal to noise sandman
written and illustrated a harvey pantera

and alph art award winning comic novel
cages

designed illustrated and photographed
bill bruford bill laswell michael nyman fear factory skinny puppy tori amos frontline
over 150 cd covers and created imagery
assembly toad the wet sprocket counting crows dream theater alice cooper machine head
and designs for ad campaigns and
nike kodak british telecom eurostar 3dfx voodoo smirnoff and bmw mini
magazines
new yorker mojo playboy penthouse blur
he runs the feral records label with top

saxophonist iain ballamy and has

directed several short film and video
the week before neon lowcraft izzy raindance buckethead bbc sonnet 138
projects

he has illustrated 3 books for children
the day i swapped my dad for 2 goldfish
written by neil gaiman and has worked
the wolves in the walls coraline
on film and book projects with iain
the falconer asylum
sinclair john cale the rolling stones
landors tower slow chocolate autopsy
jonathan carroll and stephen king
whats welsh for zen voodoo lounge black cocktail wizard + glass
he is currently writing a feature film

screenplay for channel 4, concept
the neon moth

designing for the second harry potter

film and working on a major

retrospective book due out in 2002
simplicity/complexity/complicity
occasionally he has the time to sleep

and use punctuation

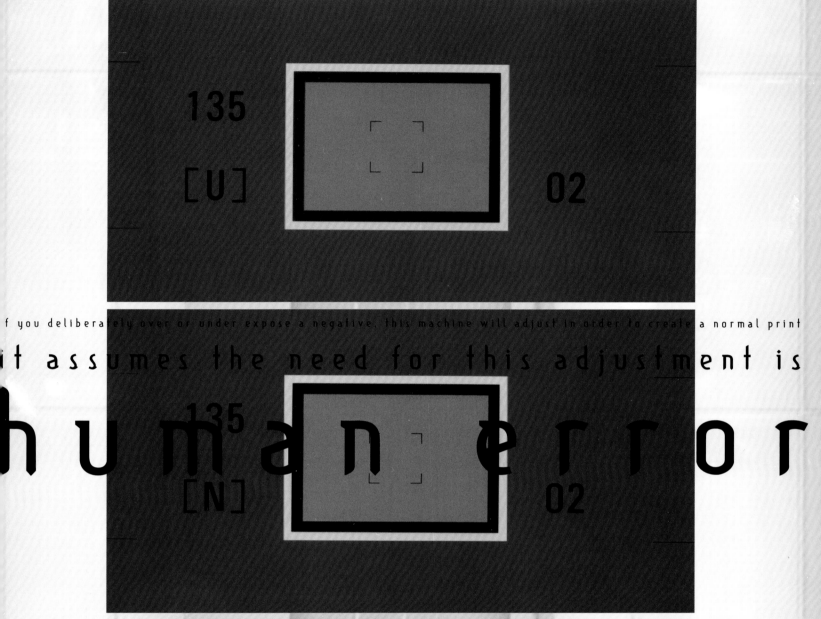

135

[U]

02

if you deliberately over or under expose a negative, this machine will adjust in order to create a normal print

it assumes the need for this adjustment is

human error

135

[N]

02

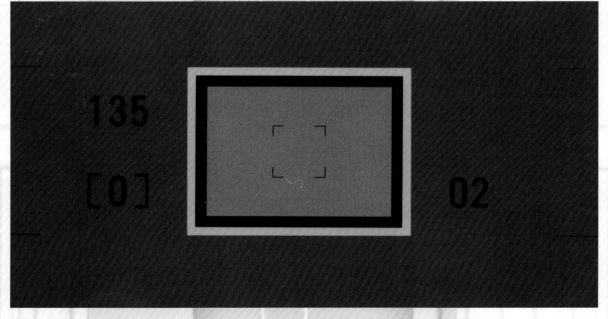

135

[O]

02

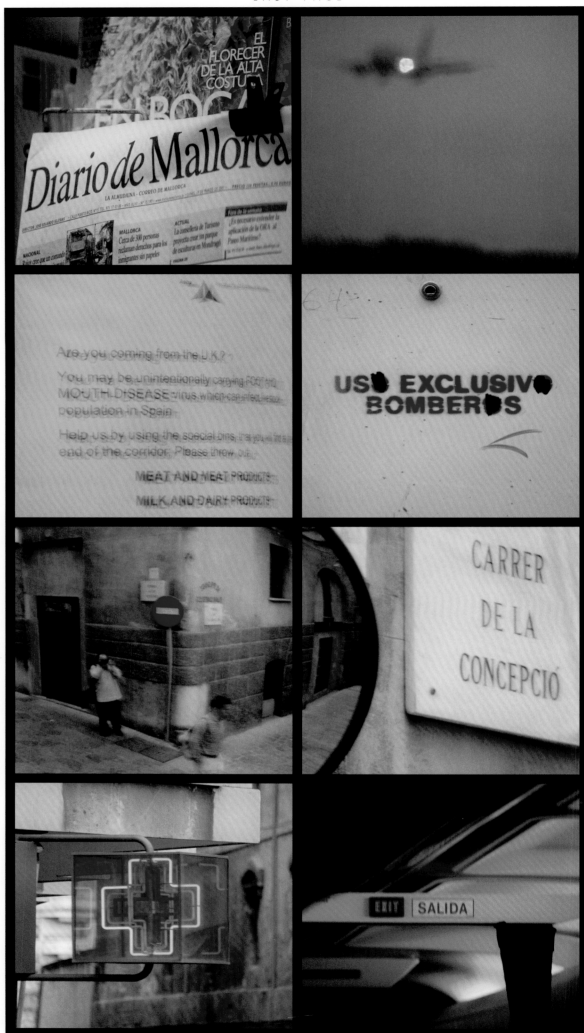